OZ ROCK
A Rock Climber's Guide to Australian Crags

Slaughterhouse Five (15), Whitewater Wall, the Freycinet Peninsula, Tasmania
Photo: Kate Chappell

OZ ROCK

A rock Climber's Guide to Australian Crags

by

ALASTAIR LEE

CICERONE PRESS

MILNTHORPE, CUMBRIA, ENGLAND

ISBN 1 85284 237 7
A catalogue record for this book is available from the British Library

For cousin Mandy

Acknowledgements

I hope this book allows many to experience the wonders and delights of climbing and travelling in what truly is a remarkable country. The following people are greatly thanked for their help towards the making of this book: Dave Allen & family; Alon Hod; Max Bretherton; Simon Bell; Keith & Kate from Tasmania; Damian Auton; Steve Saunders; Lars Olsen; Aunty Marilyn; Jean & Mike from Perth; Klaus Klein; Toby; Dale; Dave Lee; Jason Dutoit; Warick Williams; Garry Phillips; Broyan Burt; the beautiful Rachel Mitson and not forgetting my ever supportive parents, Ralph and Sylvia.

WARNING

Rock climbing is dangerous. The author and publisher accept no responsibility for inaccurate or incomplete information, nor for any controversial grading of climbs or fixed protection, some of which may be unreliable. Rock climbing in Australia is a relatively new sport. Many of the climbs are in remote places and rescue may be a long time coming and difficult to effect. Cliff rescue is not developed to anything comparable to rescue in other places of the world.

   This guide also presumes that users have a high level of ability, have received training from a skilled rock climbing instructor, will properly use appropriate equipment and have care for personal safety. The author accepts no liability or responsibility for injuries incurred due to the use of this book. Remember, climbing is a dangerous sport and you do it because you want to and at your own risk.

Front cover: The author seconds Phatang (17), Frog Buttress, Queensland.
Photo: Max Bretherton

CONTENTS

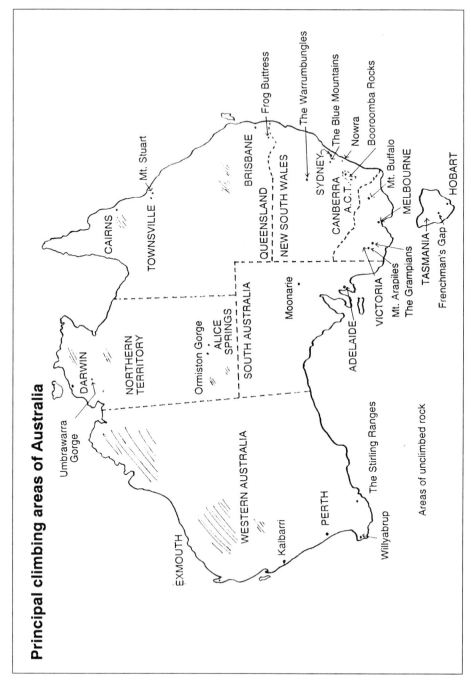

Principal climbing areas of Australia

INTRODUCTION

Australia, Rolf Harris, didgeridoos and an all but extinct indigenous race. As a rock climber you may wonder what this country could possibly have to offer you?

Where shall I start? The burning red sandstone of Arapiles, standing in open plains as far as the eye can see, the magnificent granite walls and tors raised high into the crisp and clear air of Mount Buffalo plateau, the cracked rhyolite of Mount French overlooking the peaceful pastures of southern Queensland. Perhaps the multitude of cliffs and valleys under the haze of the Blue Mountains will suit you or the amazing geological formations of the Flinders Ranges with not a soul in sight. There are sea cliffs and gorges, crags on outcrops in the arid deserts of the Red Centre. Australia is a country with some exceptional rock. This combines wonderfully with the nature that is uniquely Australian. From 10m sport routes to 800m adventure climbs, a wallaby may hop by or a wedge tailed eagle hover above. It's a land of outstanding beauty in flora and fauna where the contrast in colours and formation will startle you.

CLIMBING AREAS OF AUSTRALIA (*map 1*)

BACKGROUND/HISTORY TO AUSTRALIAN CLIMBING

Rock climbing is a relatively new activity in Australia, although earliest ascents can be dated back to the 1930's. There has been a huge acceleration in development of existing and new climbing areas over the last 10 years. The snowball continues to roll to this day and shows no sign of slowing. The list of names that have gone into this advance in Australian climbing is too long to mention, but some of the more well known stars include Malcolm Matheson, Kim Carrigan, Mike Law, Chris Baxter, Glenn Tempest, Steve Monks, Louise Shepherd, Colin Reece, Mark Moorhead, Rod Young, Chris Ewbank; trips from international climbers like Henry Barber and the late Wolfgang Güllich also helped push the ever rising standards of Australian climbing.

Considering the sheer size of Australia (a land area of 7,682,360 km², about 5 per cent of the world's land surface!) and the relatively small population of just under 17 million, climbing is doing fantastically well. It also stands to reason that the majority of the climbing has been developed where most of the people are - ie. around Melbourne and Sydney. It's just good fortune that this is where Australia's best rock is. Looking at the upper end of Australian climbing, for years the hardest climb in the country was Punks in the Gym, a monumental test piece by the legendary Wolfgang Güllich, first ascended in 1985. Only recently have Australian climbers managed to better this and close the gap on world standards with routes such as Sperm Bitches by Paul Westwood at Nowra in 1995. No doubt we've all heard of the legendary Mount Arapiles, hailed as 'the world's best crag', certainly Australia's finest. If you only have a short trip to Australia you might be well advised to spend all your time there. Many do, without even a day trip to the renowned rock of the close-by Grampians National Park. But for the venturesome climber, who enjoys that fine mixture of travelling the open road experiencing variety, camping and climbing in an almost wilderness environment, then moving on, Australia is a place you no longer need to dream about.

There is also a phenomenal amount of unclimbed rock, particularly in Western Australia, but there are reasons for this - approach roads of hundreds of kilometres in dry, hostile conditions. If you do decide to develop a new area then always contact the local authorities, eg. the ranger for a given national park, to get permission to climb and find out what the local ethics on bolting are for a given area. There can be a dramatic difference in views towards climbing from one national park to another. Some have a total ban on climbing, whereas others encourage bolting for safety reasons.

NATURAL HAZARDS/SAFETY FIRST

Bushfires - Due to the very hot and dry patches of weather in most parts of Australia at certain times of the year, there is a very high risk of a 'bushfire'. Extra caution must be taken whenever open fires or stoves are in use. Indeed on some days of particular high risk a total fire ban is put in place throughout the state, where it is an offence to allow any naked flame. News broadcasts and keeping in regular contact with the ranger will help notify you of these days. On any camping trip always pack some food that does not require the use of a stove to eat for such occasions.

Fire safety
Never leave a fire unattended.
Always use marked fire places, if provided.
Keep all inflammable substances well away from fire.
Ensure fire is fully extinguished before going to bed.

The Sun - Another natural hazard to be aware of in Australia is the danger of the sun. Australia currently holds the highest rate of skin cancer in the world, making protection from the sun's rays an essential part of anyone's preparations before setting out for the crag. Sunburn can occur within 15 minutes of exposure in some parts of Australia, therefore wearing a wide brimmed hat (very important for belayers), staying covered with lightweight clothing and the use of a high factor sun cream are recommended. A good supply of drinking water is also a wise move for climbing at Australian crags.

Snakes - Australia has over one hundred species of snakes, twenty-five of which may be considered dangerous. One of these, the Small-scaled or Fierce snake, is branded as the world's most venomous! Generally speaking, however, snakes are very shy creatures and if the following advice is adopted your chances of being bitten will be greatly reduced. First of all, most Australian snakes do not act aggressively unless provoked; only if cornered, struck or trodden upon may they attack. Therefore, if you are confronted by a snake do not make any attempt to touch or prod it, simply remaining calm and walking away is all that is required to avoid being bitten in most cases. A typical snake's habitat would be long grassy areas, bushlands, leaves or other rotting foliage, under logs and fallen trees and occasionally under, in or behind rocks! Be particularly cautious in this type of terrain, where keeping to footpaths and not poking about in the undergrowth are both well advised, as is a torch for late evenings. All Australian snakes, other than the Death Adder, will retreat (if they are awake) when they detect the vibrations of human movement. Stamping your feet to warn snakes of your presence (not shouting as snakes are totally deaf) is a good practice if you think you are in an area of significant danger. Snakes hibernate in winter. If you do come across a sleeping snake be careful not to wake it as they can quickly become active and attack.

Bites most commonly occur on the foot, ankle or hand. If you are unfortunate enough to be bitten, then try to remain calm and follow this simple first aid procedure:

THE PRESSURE/IMMOBILISATION METHOD

Pressure: Without unclothing apply a firm dressing over the bitten area, tightly covering as much area as possible.

Immobilise: Do not move the bitten area. Apply a splint to an ankle bite and use a sling for a bite to the hand or arm.

The philosophy behind this is to stop any venom spreading away from the bitten area and attacking major organs in the body.

Also try to remember the snake's appearance (ie. colour, pattern and size) as this will help doctors select the correct anti-venom for the bite. This first aid method can be used for any bite or sting you may incur while in Australia.

Other poisonous land creatures to be aware of include the Red-backed spider, the Sydney Funnel-web spider, centipedes and scorpions. Treat these creatures with respect. Avoid untouched dark corners and always check under the toilet seat!

9

In the event of a bite from a snake, spider or anything you suspect to be venomous always seek medical advice.

Crocodiles - Not wanting to cause any undue alarm, it should also be noted that rivers and estuaries in northern parts of Australia contain man eating crocodiles. Check with the locals about the crocodile situation before swimming in any water.

The Tropics - When in the Tropics pay special attention to any cuts and abrasions sustained. Because of the high temperatures wounds easily become infected. Always treat any opening of the skin with antiseptic lotion.

Environmental care - Australia's crags are some of the most beautiful in the world. They are a fine example of how climbing areas should be treated. Always take your rubbish home with you, never mark or deface the rock in any way and if toilets are not available, then deal with human waste in the correct manner, by burying it at least 15cm under the ground and 50m away from any water supply. The cliffs and the land around them are fragile areas. Only by acting considerately will we preserve their beauty for future generations to enjoy. Always check the park rules with regard to 'flora & fauna'. Acting responsibly towards the native environment should be your duty as a climber. Not caring for crags risks everybody's climbing future in Australia.

Safety first

In case of emergency dial 000.

Taking the sheer size of Australia into consideration, it stands to reason that any rescue operation, particularly for crags which are located further afield (eg. Moonarie, some 50km from the nearest major town - Port Augusta, with an hour's hike from car park to cliff), is going to be a lengthy ordeal in the case of a serious accident. Cliff rescue has not developed to the same extent as in other parts of the world. Bearing all this in mind, always use good judgement, be self preservative and take great care when climbing in Australia.

ACCOMMODATION/TRANSPORTATION GUIDE

Australia is a country of enormous size, comparable with that of Western Europe or Continental America. On a map of equal scale countries such as Japan or the United Kingdom would look to be merely surrounding islands in comparison with the imposing mass of Australia. If you plan to travel extensively, be prepared for some long journeys. The well known drive across the Nullabar from Adelaide to Perth may involve 3 or 4 days' driving or a rather unpleasant 35 hours on a bus. The main options you have are public transport (bus or train) or buying a vehicle.

Car hire, flying and hitching are of course all viable options. (Hitching in Australia, as with anywhere in the world, can be very dangerous, particularly, but not only for women.) National coach networks offer good deals for travellers in the form of passes. They are also a safe comfortable means of getting about. The major drawback with public transport, however, is that you can often only get as close to a crag as the nearest town, leaving you between 10 and 50km off target. If travelling alone, a good way of overcoming this is to pay the local climbing gym a visit (addresses of which are given). By meeting other climbers, a lift to the crag and a partner for the day can easily be arranged.

For a stay of 3 months or longer, where a list of crags is on the itinerary, buying a vehicle is probably the best option. A van or station wagon you can sleep in will help out accommodation costs and prove more convenient. This will allow you complete freedom of movement and access to the remotest of climbing spots. Driving around Australia (on the left-hand side of the road) can be a very pleasurable affair. Be warned, however, that if you intend to travel in the outback, particularly Western Australia, long distances lie between some towns. Checking weather conditions, being familiar with your vehicle and carrying spare parts and supplies of food and water are standard practice for these trips. In the Northern Territory, during heavy rainfall in the 'wet season' (Oct-Mar), roads can become impassable. Obtain information on road conditions from tourist information centres (addresses given) before departure.

For most of the major crags in Australia, good camping facilities are available and are either free or very reasonably priced. (Camping at crags is indicated.) Australia is a well facilitated country towards tourist and traveller. All cities and most towns have a variety of budget accommodation in the form of 'backpackers' and hostels. You would be very unfortunate to find a town in Australia without one of the establishments, as hostelling is a well publicised and flourishing industry.

USE OF GUIDEBOOK

Although every effort has been made to ensure that the information given in this book is as accurate as possible, new crags open and old crags close, so inevitably there will be errors! This is the biggest collection of Australian crags inside one cover and the first book to look at climbing in Australia as a whole at the time of publishing. It by no means claims to list every climbing area in Australia. The intention of the guide is to point out the major crags of Australia and some of the not so major ones; to give the reader an overview of where the climbing is and what each location is like. The book will tell you what type of climbing you can expect, what the rock is and the quality of it, the protection you will require, the number of climbs and the length of the climbs. A few classic climbs are recommended where applicable and the author also gives an overall rating of each crag.

Rock quality: This is graded from poor, fair, sound, good to excellent. This is to give an indication of the fragility or solidness of the rock. Poor meaning lots of loose rocks, holds often breaking, the rock being of a very brittle composition. Excellent means the rock is of a very solid nature and holds breaking unheard of.

Grade of climbs: This is the range of grades you can expect to find at any given crag (the remarks in brackets refer to what most climbs are).

Length of climbs: This is the range of length of climbs you can expect to find at any given crag (a remark of either single or multi-pitch, and sometimes both, refers to the majority of climbs at any given crag).

SPORT: This symbol means that 'sport climbing' is possible at the given crag.

Location and access: Don't be misled by the term 'Main Highway' as in almost all cases these are two way traffic roads (single lane in each direction). Freeways are the equivalent of British motorways. All directions (left and right) are given facing the cliff.

What to take: It is assumed that any climber has a basic set up of climbing equipment including: a 50m rope, harnesses, boots, chalk bag, 4 locking crabs, 6 or so slings, a full set of quick draws and 10 bolt plates.

Author's rating:

    *   A good crag, recommended

    **   Highly recommended

    ***   Don't miss it!

This is specific to the mentioned area and style of climbing.

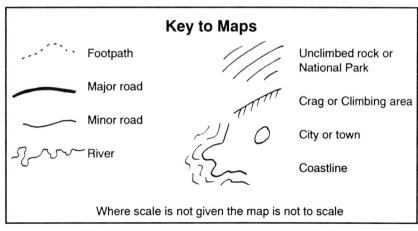

Key to Maps

Footpath

Major road

Minor road

River

Unclimbed rock or National Park

Crag or Climbing area

City or town

Coastline

Where scale is not given the map is not to scale

GRADE COMPARISON TABLE

Australian	American	British		French	UIAA
14	5.7	VS	4a	4	5
15		VS	4b	4	5+
16	5.8	HVS	4c	5	6-
17	5.9	E1	5a	5	6
18	5.10a	E1	5b	6a	6+
19	5.10b	E2	5b	6a	7-
20	5.10c	E2	5c	6b	7
21	5.10d	E2	5c	6b	7
22	5.11a / 5.11b	E3	6a	6c	7+
23	5.11c	E3	6a	6c	8-
24	5.11d	E4	6a	7a	8
25	5.12a	E4	6a	7a	8+
26	5.12b	E5	6b	7b	9-
27	5.12c / 5.12d	E5	6b	7b	9
28	5.13a	E6	6c	7c	9+
29	5.13b	E7	6c	8a	10-
30	5.13c	E7	7a	8b	10
31	5.13d	E8	7a	8b	10
32	5.14a	E8	7b	8c	10+
33	5.14b / 5.14c	E9	7b	8c	11-
34	5.14d	E9	7c	9a	11

A useful conversion 1km = 0.62137   1 mile = 1.60934kms

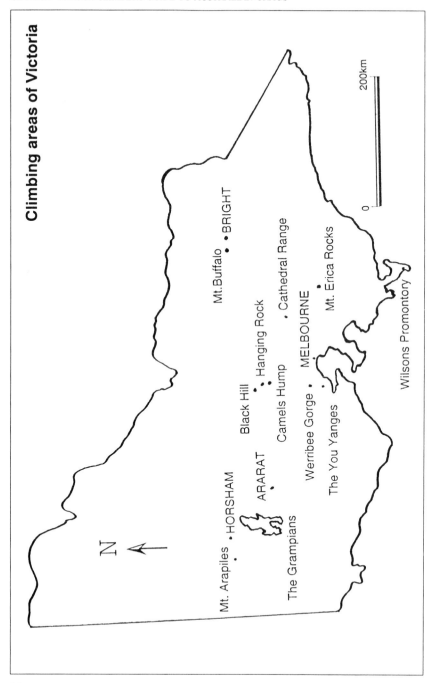

Climbing areas of Victoria

VICTORIA

Victoria is one of mainland Australia's smallest states. Its fertile, picturesque lands offer incredible natural beauty. It also hosts some of Australia's best climbing.

MOUNT ARAPILES

At 3km in length standing 150m clear of the surrounding Wimmera wetlands, this cliff is an outstanding rock venue. Its gullies, walls and buttresses, all in orange quartzitic sandstone make a perfect climbing arena. Hundreds of classic lines grace this cliff, whether it be the gymnastic moves of a world class route or the traditional exertion of a glorious multi-pitch. Both will be equally high in quality. Easily accessible, pleasant camping grounds, burning sunrises, kangaroos jumping by - there's no place quite like it. Any climbing trip to Australia would not be complete without experiencing the magnificence of Arapiles.

Geology: Quartz and calcite sandstone

Number of climbs: 2000+

Grade of climbs: 4-32 (All grades)

Potential for new routes: No

Rock quality: Excellent

Protection: 99% natural pro, some bolted routes

Length of climbs: 10-160m single and multi-pitch

Predominant climbing style: All styles

SPORT

Location and Access
Mount Arapiles is 300km north-west of Melbourne. Take the western highway (8) out of Melbourne, signposted to Ballarat and Adelaide. Stay on this road for 300km until you come to the town of Horsham. Mount Arapiles is 36km directly west of Horsham via highway 130. Pass through the small town of Natimuk and the crag is clearly visible and signposted on the right-hand side 9km after this. Access to the climbs is just a few minutes' walk for the closest area from the camping ground.

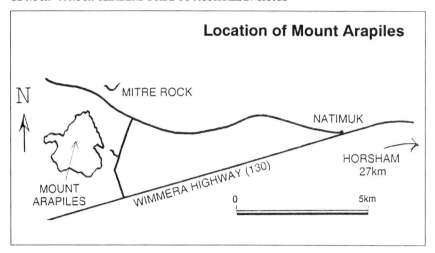

Camping and Supplies

Camping at Mount Arapiles is split into two adjacent areas named The Pines and The Gums. Facilities include toilets, water, wash basins, a shelter, litter bins, a public telephone, fireplaces and picnic tables. Camping fees apply.

The nearby town of Natimuk has a selection of facilities including a climbing shop. But if larger purchases of goods are required a trip to the town of Horsham would be more economical.

Climate and when to go

In autumn (Feb-April) and spring (Sept-Nov) conditions at Mount Arapiles are idyllic and this is the best time to go. Winter (May-Aug) can be cold, particularly at night, and summer (Dec-Jan) will be very hot. Having said that it is fairly inconceivable that you could find a time of year when there are not climbers at Mount Arapiles. These days the campsite remains at least half full all year round, just filling up on popular weekends. Make a note to avoid the masses that flock there during Christmas and New Year.

Mount Arapiles is renowned for its blue skies and low rainfall and in general this is the case. However, don't be surprised by the odd rainy day, particularly in autumn, and watch out for prevailing winds across the plains which can make the evenings a little cool.

What to take

A full rack of natural protection including plenty of wires, SLCDs and friends. Hexes and stoppers will also come in useful. Two 50m ropes suffice for most abseils. For late autumn or winter trips a 4 season sleeping bag and a good tent are essential. A stove for cooking as firewood is limited.

Mount Buffalo, north side of the gorge, Victoria. Photo: Klaus Klein

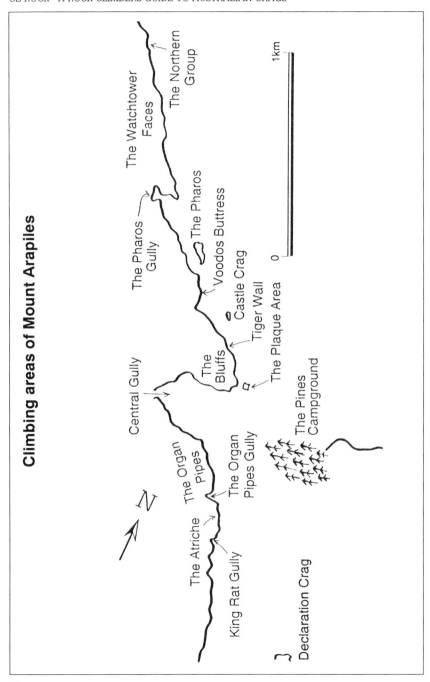

Climbing areas of Mount Arapiles

The Watchtower Faces

The Northern Group

The Pharos Gully

The Pharos

Voodos Buttress

Castle Crag

Tiger Wall

The Plaque Area

Central Gully

The Bluffs

The Organ Pipes

The Organ Pipes Gully

The Pines Campground

The Atriche

King Rat Gully

Declaration Crag

N

0   1km

Alon Hod leads Kachoong (21), Mount Arapiles. Photo: Alastair Lee

Recommended classics

Little Thor	12m	20	(Declaration Crag)
D Minor	33m	14	(The Organ Pipes)
Checkmate	117m	17	(Bard Buttress)
Anxiety Neurosis	40m	26	(The Bluffs)
Phoenix	93m	11	(Tiger Wall)
Judgement Day	111m	20	(The Pharos)
The Siren	163m	7	(The Pinnacle Face)
Auto de Fé	90m	21	(The Watchtower Faces)
Cliff Hanger	25m	24	(The Northern Group)
Orestes	40m	24	(The Atridae)
Los Endos	40m	22	(Central Gully right side)
The Bard	120m	12	(Bard Buttress)
India	25m	29	(The Pharos)
Birdman of Alcatraz	36m	23	(The Pharos)
Punks in the Gym	20m	32	(The Pharos)
The Watchtower Crack	100m	16	
Kachoong	25m	21	(The Northern Group)

Alon Hod on the distinctive bulging rock of Mount Arapiles. Photo: Alastair Lee

Bouldering

Arapiles is renowned for its hundreds of fine lines of all lengths and grades. What should also be noted is the great bouldering on offer. What better way to finish a day's climbing than an hour's fun on the golden boulders of Arapiles. Look out for the area in front of the central gully, Rabbit boulder, Declaration crag and for more strenuous problems The Torture Chambers on the upper right-hand side of central gully.

Useful numbers

Ambulance: 82 222

Natimuk hospital: 871 205

Natimuk police: 871 280

Arapiles rescue: 871 492; 871 505 or 871 515

Author's rating ***

Guide to climbs

A Rock Climber's Guide to Arapiles/Djurite by Louise Shepherd (1994)

THE GRAMPIANS

The Grampians is a spectacular national park. Steep jagged mountains in rugged terrain cover some 2000km². The opposing sandstone ranges stretch 100km across the land. High escarpments and peaks scatter cliffs and outcrops throughout. On the 150 or so developed climbing areas within the Grampians the rock varies from simple grey to the classic red/orange Arapiles type of sandstone. There are thousands of climbs to choose from, incorporating the diversity of all rock climbing styles and every type of route imaginable.

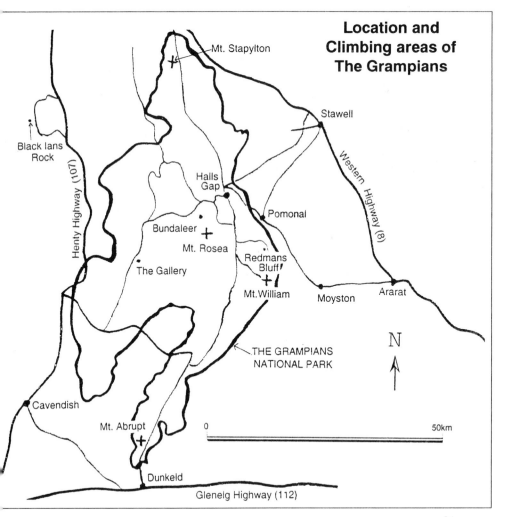

Location and Climbing areas of The Grampians

Geology: Sandstone

Number of climbs: 2000+

Grade of climbs: 5-30 (all grades)

Potential for new routes: Yes

Rock quality: Good

Protection: Bolts and natural pro

Length of climbs: 10-240m single and multi-pitch

Predominant climbing style: Steep faces, overhangs and cracks

SPORT

Location and Access

The Grampians are to be found about 250km north-west of Melbourne, lying between the Western and Glenelg highways. The park can be accessed from all directions, depending on where you intend to climb. The most popular route is to go along the Western Highway to Ararat, turning left here to go through Mogston and Pomanal and arrive at Halls Gap. Most of the better known crags (but not all) are a short drive from here. Most of the cliffs are within 10 to 30 minutes' walk from a parking spot, the network of winding roads within the park making even the remotest of places accessible.

Camping and Supplies

There are many campsites in the Grampians national park, official and unofficial. On the official campsites toilets, water and fire places can be found and fees are applicable. One exception is the Mount Difficult plantation site which has all the above facilities but is free as it lies just outside the national park. Unofficial camping grounds can be found by the sides of lots of the crags, in more natural scrub bush-like surroundings. Sites of this nature require drinking water to be carried in and remember to take great care with any open fires.

Although the Grampians has its own town (Halls Gap) which has all the usual amenities you will find in a small town (supermarket, banks, etc.) goods are quite expensive. It is cheaper to stock up with food for your trip in one of the larger towns of Ararat, Stowell or Horsham.

Climate and when to go

The weather at the Grampians is very similar to that of Mount Arapiles. The best times to go are spring (Sept-Nov) and autumn (Mar-May). Because of the Grampians' slightly higher altitude, nights can get quite cool and on the higher peaks snow is not unheard of. Year round climbing is possible, however. Many winter days blow clear with milder temperatures. Summers are hot and unless you have a fetish for slimy holds, climbing in the shade is required.

22

The Grampians from Mount Abrupt. Photo: Alastair Lee

What to take

A full rack of wires, friends, quickdraws, slings and some bolt hangers. If you don't have any natural gear there are some purely bolted sport routes, particularly at The Gallery climbing area. Double ropes for some of the more indirect lines will pay high dividends. For getting to and accessing the crags in the national park your own transport is essential. Don't attempt to climb the Grampians by public transport! A 10 litre water container comes in useful for any stay in the more remote camping areas.

Classic cliffs

In the north look out for the amazing Taipan wall at Mount Stapylton. More central are perhaps two of the best, certainly most popular cliffs, Bandaleer and Mount Rosea. For some of Victoria's top sport climbing don't miss The Gallery. For adventure climbing with superb exposure, then pay Redmans Bluff a visit. Other outstanding cliffs include Eureka Wall, Green Gap Pinnacle, Emu Rock, The Fortress, Tortoise Wall, The Breach and The Temple.

10km north-west of the park lies some excellent climbing on the popular and compact cliff of Black Ions Rocks.

Useful numbers

National park headquarters: (053) 56 4381   Halls Gap police: (053) 56 4411
Cliff rescue: 87 1492; 87 1505 or 87 1515

The author checks the view from Mount Abrupt, The Grampians. Photo: Jon

Author's rating *

Guide to climbs

A Rock Climber's Guide to the North Grampians by Bill Andrews (Victoria Climbing Club Inc.)
Rock Climbs of Halls Gap and the Wonderland Range by Bill Andrews (VCC)
South-eastern Grampians by Chris Baxter (VCC)
The Victoria Range by Kieran Loughran (VCC)

MOUNT BUFFALO

Mount Buffalo is undoubtedly Australia's major granite climbing venue. Set high on a 1500m plateau, the solid tors, immense boulders and gorges give a perfect vantage point to see the splendour of the surrounding alpine land. So crisp and clear is the Mount Buffalo air, it is quite refreshing. The unique vegetation combined with stunning rock formation make it a joy to be in such a place.

The climbing at Mount Buffalo is simply magnificent. Gigantic slabs of featureless faces beckon the climber to experience the vast and enthralling exposure. Fantastic lines slice through stone monuments from base to summit. The length and endurance will test anyone's rock climbing ability to the limit. For

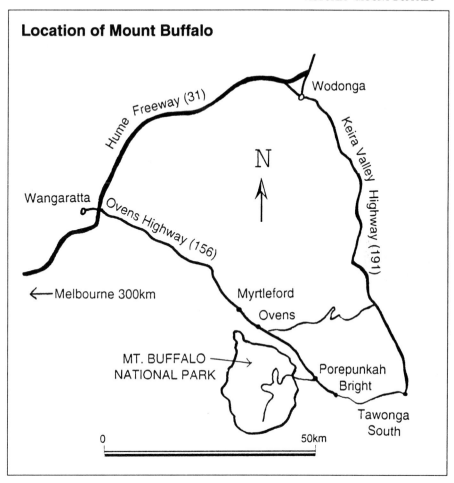

Location of Mount Buffalo

the more traditional enthusiast seeking a long adventure type of climbing, the serious nature and demanding aspects of Buffalo climbs will not disappoint.

Geology: Granite

Number of climbs: 200+

Grade of climbs: 15-29

Potential for new routes: Yes

Rock quality: Excellent

Protection: Natural pro and bolts

Length of climbs: 15-280m single and multi-pitch

Predominant climbing style: Slab, face and cracks

SPORT

25

Location and Access

Mount Buffalo is located about 300km north-east of Melbourne. From either Melbourne, Sydney or Canberra, the best approach is the Hume Freeway to Wangaratta, then the Ovens highway will lead you to the small town of Porepunkah. 20km of road takes you up to the plateau from here. Mount Buffalo being a major attraction is a well signposted national park. Trains and buses also run regularly to Wangaratta, where you can catch a not so regular bus to the national park.

Access to the cliffs at Mount Buffalo varies from a 10 minute walk to sites like The Cathedral and The Horn to a 3 hour commando style approach of bush bashing and river crossing to reach the base of the Mount McCloud slabs. For the routes in the gorge, a series of abseils is required.

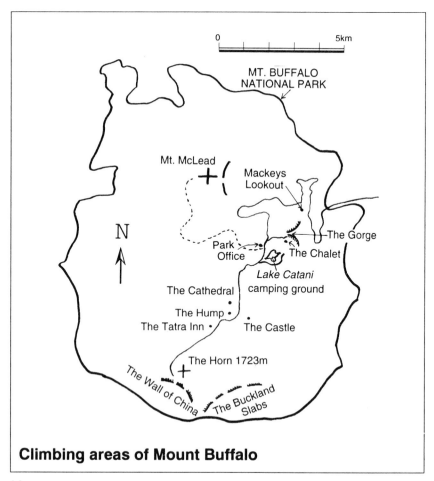

Climbing areas of Mount Buffalo

Camping and Supplies

There is only one campsite on the plateau, situated at Lake Catani and open Dec-Apr. The site is stringently run by the park rangers. Tent sites are numbered and expensive. If you intend to use the site, then you are strongly advised to book in advance, particularly at the peak times of Dec-Jan when places are hard to come by. The campsite offers excellent facilities in the form of hot showers, toilets and firewood. If the campsite is full, then one option would be to crag commute from a campsite at one of the nearby towns of Porepunkah or Eurobin. A national park fee is also payable on entrance.

Get well supplied with foods and fuels before going up to Mount Buffalo at one of the approaching towns (Wangaratta, Myottford). There is no petrol station on the plateau and food is only available at the two expensive café type establishments.

Climate and when to go

During the winter months (May-Sept) Mount Buffalo will be found under several layers of snow and turns into a ski resort, so climbing is definitely out. Summer (Nov-Jan) is the most popular and best time to go because of the comparatively mild temperature and perfect clear skies. Spring and autumn are viable options with good weather often blessing both seasons, with clear skies. The days are fresh and nights cold, frosts being the norm.

What to take

For the longer climbs in the gorge 2 x 50m ropes are essential. Full rack of wires and lots of large friends and 10 or so bolt hangers. The rock at Mount Buffalo can be quite coarse so plenty of tape to protect your hands whilst jamming is a wise precaution. Good sturdy walking boots for some of the longer approach routes. Thermals and waterproofs along with food and water in your day pack on longer climbs as the weather can be changeable.

Recommended classics

There are 11 developed climbing areas at Mount Buffalo, more popular ones include The Gorge, The Cathedral, The Hump, The Horn and The Buckland Slabs. Recommended climbs include:

Where angels fear to tread	228m	17	(south side of the gorge)
Hard Rain	118m	22M1	(south side of the gorge)
Rough Justice	157m	28	(north side of the gorge)
El Supremo	157m	25	(north side of the gorge)

At the bottom of the gorge look out for a 30m 25 on the False Modesty Pinnacle

Sultan	65m	21	(The Cathedral)
The Dreaming	75m	23	(The Cathedral)
The Edge of Pleasure	75m	21	(The Cathedral)
A Star is Born	55m	19	(The Buckland Slabs)

Useful numbers
Park ranger (campsite booking, rescue and weather update): (057) 55 1577
Head ranger: (057) 55 1466

Author's rating *

Guide to climbs
'Mount Buffalo': a Rock Climber's Guide by Jeremy Boreham and David Brereton (VCC, 1996)

The principal climbing areas of Victoria have been covered. There are, however, many smaller developed crags around the Melbourne region, all making feasible day trips from the city. If you do get stuck in the city with only the odd day off, these are perfect opportunities to get away from it all and climb in some lovely locations.

THE YOU YANGS

Geology: Granite

Number of climbs: 400+

Grade of climbs: 10-28 (mostly middle grade)

Potential for new routes: No

Rock quality: Sound, very sharp

Protection: Mainly bolts, some natural

Length of climbs: 10-32m single pitch

Predominant climbing style: Slab

SPORT

Location and Access
Take the Princess highway 60km south-west of Melbourne, heading for Geelong, exit at Little River. Go through the town and follow the signs for 10km to the park, where an entrance fee is payable.

The granite boulders can be found throughout the park. A circular gravel track allows easy access to all climbing areas.

Author's rating *

Guide to climbs
The You Yangs: An annotated list of rock climbs compiled by Ken Jones and Ken Wheat (1993)

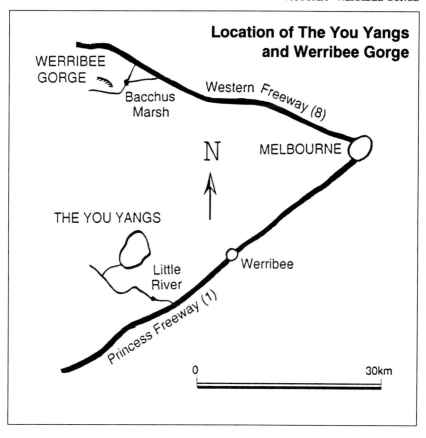

Location of The You Yangs and Werribee Gorge

WERRIBEE GORGE

Bacchus Marsh

Western Freeway (8)

N

MELBOURNE

THE YOU YANGS

Little River

Werribee

Princess Freeway (1)

0   30km

WERRIBEE GORGE

Geology: Conglomerate sandstone

Number of climbs: 50

Grade of climbs: 10-26 (Good selection of all grades)

Potential for new routes: No

Rock quality: Sound (watch for loose rock near the top)

Protection: Bolts and natural pro

Length of climbs: 10-30m single pitch

Predominant climbing style: Steep crack and face climbs

SPORT

Location and Access

The gorge is situated 70km west of Melbourne. Take the Western Freeway to Bacchus Marsh. From here turn left leading to Geelong. Turn right before the railway line onto Griffiths Street. After 2km turn right onto McCormacks Road then turn right again after the bridge onto Bullen Road. The now dirt road continues alongside the railway line. When the road crosses the line, look for a place to park by the fence. From here it's about 30 minutes' walk over the stile and on the track across the fields. When you reach the Werribee Gorge State Park follow the track left down to the cliff top. Abseil down from here using the fixed anchors provided.

Guide to climbs

Melbourne's Best by Michael Hampton (Wild Publication, 1995)

BLACK HILL

Geology: Granite

Number of climbs: 100+

Grade of climbs: 16-26

Potential for new routes: No

Rock quality: Sound, can be sharp

Protection: Mainly bolts, natural pro required on some routes

Length of climbs: 15-130m mainly single but a few multi-pitch

Predominant climbing style: Face

SPORT

Location and Access

From Melbourne head north-west on the Calder highway. 5km after Gisborne turn right onto the Mount Macedon Road. In 3km turn left at the Memorial Cross lookout sign. Follow this road for

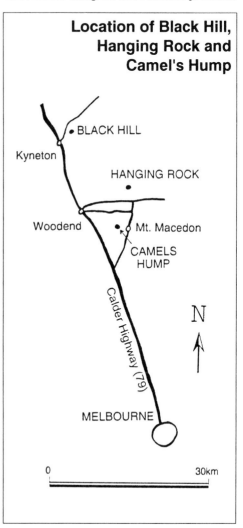

Location of Black Hill, Hanging Rock and Camel's Hump

a short distance to the car park. The main climbing is at an area called The Omega Block and can be found by following the walking track, turning down the left branch and passing through some boulders.

Author's rating *

Guide to climbs
As above.

HANGING ROCK

Geology: Volcanic

Number of climbs: 100

Grade of climbs: 5-29 (mainly middle grade)

Potential for new routes: No

Rock quality: Fair

Protection: Bolts and natural gear

Length of climbs: 10-60m mainly single pitch

Predominant climbing style: Face (often steep)

SPORT

Location and Access
Drive 80km north-west on the Calder Highway from Melbourne to Woodend. Exit the highway 1km after this and follow the signs to Hanging Rock. Park fees are payable. To reach the climbs follow the summit track to the steps; climbing can be found left and right of this point.

Guide to climbs
As above.

THE CATHEDRAL RANGE

Geology: Sandstone

Number of climbs: 150

Grade of climbs: 3-24 (middle/easy grades)

Potential for new routes: No

Rock quality: Sound

Protection: Few bolts, mainly natural pro

Length of climbs: 15-150m single and multi-pitch

Predominant climbing style: High angle slabs

SPORT

Location and Access

Take the Maroondah highway (34) north-east form Melbourne 120km to Buxton. About 10km after Buxton, take a right turn down Cathedral Lane. After a few more km turn right into Cathedral Range State Park. Three climbing areas can be accessed by parking across from the Neds Gully campsite. The most popular and best climbing is found on the North Jawbones. To reach this area continue along the track to the Cooks Mill campsite, then up the hill to park on the right. The North Jawbones can be seen from here.

Author's rating *

Guide to climbs

Eastern District Guide by Glenn Tempest and Richard Smith (1988)

MOUNT ERICA ROCKS

Geology: Granite

Number of climbs: 70

Grade of climbs: 10-25 (middle grade)

Potential for new routes: No

Rock quality: Sound

Protection: Mainly bolts, some natural pro

Length of climbs: 10-35m single pitch

Predominant climbing style: Slabs, faces, arêtes

SPORT

There is excellent bouldering at Mount Erica Rocks.

Location and Access

Mount Erica Rocks are 180km east of Melbourne in the Bow Bow National Park. Head south east out of Melbourne on the Princess Highway (1) to Moe. From here take the north road to Erica and roughly 10km later there is a dirt track, signposted to Mount Erica on the left. This will take you to a car park. Take the walking track to the boulder field from here.

Guide to climbs

As above.

Kim Mckeown on Buandick, The Grampians, Victoria *Photo Klaus Klein*
Andrew Dunbar on Kachoong (21), Mount Arapiles, Victoria *Photo Klaus Klein*

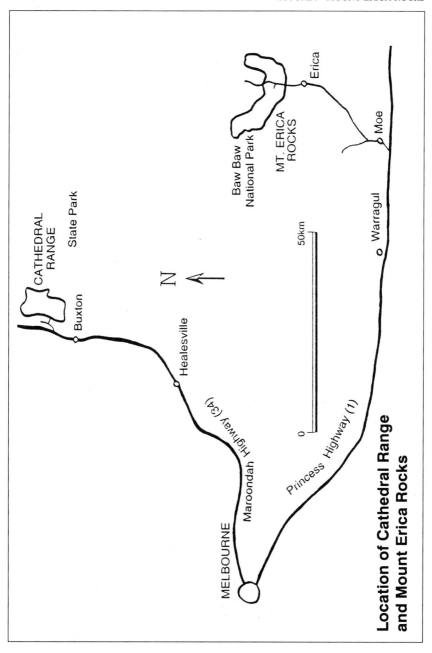

Location of Cathedral Range and Mount Erica Rocks

Chancellor Direct (17), The Organ Pipes, Tasmania. Photo: Kate Chappell

WILSONS PROMONTORY

Geology: Granite

Number of climbs: 150

Grade of climbs: 15-25 (middle grade)

Potential for new routes: No

Rock quality: Good

Protection: Natural pro

Length of climbs: 30-120m single and multi-pitch

Predominant climbing style: Slabs (sea cliffs)

Location and Access

Take the Princess Highway 250km south-east from Melbourne to Dandenong. From here take Hwy 180 all the way to Meeniyan, passing through Korumburra and Leongatha. From Meeniyan pass through Fish Creek and follow signs to Wilsons Promontory National Park. Entrance fees are payable.

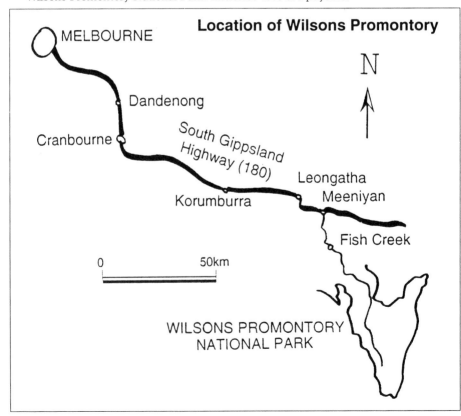

Popular areas include Whale Rock, Mount Bishop and Mount Oberon and are around 30 minutes' walking. There is also excellent bouldering at Squeaky and Whisky beaches.

Camping is allowed within the park.

Useful numbers

Park ranger: (056) 80 9555

Guide to climbs

Eastern District Guide by Glenn Tempest and Richard Smith (1988)

BOULDERING - BURNLEY BRIDGE

If you're stuck in Melbourne and itching to climb then have a look under the Burnley bridge in the suburb of Burnley, near Richmond. It's a concrete flyover, adjacent to the River Yarra which has been claimed by devotees of large forearms as a steep and difficult training area. Holds are glued, chipped and decorated with graffiti. However after a few days of the bustling business district such ethical sins are a pleasing sight. (Well, it is only the underside of a bridge!) The full traverse of about 30m is graded highly, where at the right-hand end the already overhanging path of holds continues out through a roof of man-made girders and supportive struts. Like it or pump it, this is something different.

Useful addresses

*Cliffhanger Climbing Gym Pty Ltd
Westgate Sport & Leisure Complex
Cnr Grieve Pde and Doherty's Road
Altona, North Victoria 3025
Tel (03) 369 6400
*Probably Oz's best gym!

Rockworks (gym)
Factory 1, 74 Lipton Drive
Thomastown
Victoria 3074
Tel (03) 462 4054

The Victorian Climbing Centre
Unit 1, 12 Hartnett Dve
Seaford, Victoria 3198
Tel (03) 782 4222

The Hardrock Climbing Company Pty Ltd (gym)
Unit 2, 16 Varman Crt
Nunawading, Victoria 3131
Tel (03) 894 4183

Victoria Ranges Indoor Pistol & Rock Climbing Centre
40 Mount Alexander Road
Flemington, Victoria
Tel (03) 372 2500

Geelong YMCA (gym)
78 Yarva Street
Geelong, Victoria 3220
Tel: (052) 218344

Climbatic (gym)
26 Boswell Avenue
Newtown, Victoria
Tel (052) 221684

Tourism Victoria
403 George Street
Sydney, NSW 2000
Tel (02) 299 2288

Department of Conservation and
Environment
240/250 Victoria Parade (PO Box 41)
East Melbourne, Victoria 3002
Tel (03) 412 4011
Fax (03) 412 4166

For any guidebooks or equipment you may require, there are a host of outdoor
shops, all conveniently located in Little Bourke Street, Melbourne city centre.

TASMANIA

Somewhat separated from the mainland, Tasmania has a very different landscape and climate from what is commonly thought to be Australian. There are rich, fertile, undulating lands to the north, fierce and rugged mountain wildernesses to the largely untouched south-west. With consistent rainfall, mild summers, cold winters and a prevailing wind from the roaring forties, a climbing trip to Tasmania is definitely not for the faint hearted. There is the usual spread of single pitch sports

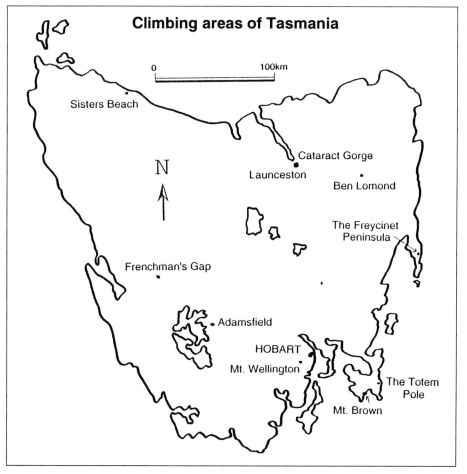

Climbing areas of Tasmania

crags which are commonplace in today's climbing world, so why bother with the trip over the Bass strait, you might ask. The answer is Australia's longest climbs, with stunning peaks and rock formations of a beauty that only the wild and remote southern parks of Tasmania could create. There are expedition type trips with 1 or 2 days' approach through untouched bushland, testing your skills and endurance in a harsh environment where the weather may dictate success. This is Alpine climbing Australian style!

FRENCHMAN'S CAP

Perhaps Australia's premier Alpine rockclimbing area, the routes are long and serious affairs. The prize of summiting the fantastic white monolith of the cap is still highly regarded. Areas require at least a day's walk, involving preparation and equipment associated more closely with an expedition. There are many factors, including extreme exposure, to be taken on board for climbing at the Frenchman's Cap. The area is very remote, the weather is unpredictably changeable. Routes have had only a few ascents. They are long, in places loose, and can be difficult to protect. This is 'adventure climbing' for the experienced only.

Geology: Quartzite

Number of climbs: 40

Grade of climbs: 8-23 (Easy, middle grade)

Potential for new routes: Yes

Rock quality: Good (can be loose due to frost shattering)

Protection: Natural pro

Length of climbs: 30-500m, some single, mainly multi-pitch

Predominant climbing style: Multi-pitch adventure

Location and Access

Frenchman's Cap is located in the Franklin-Gordon Wild Rivers National Park, 25km off the Lyell Highway (A10), 200km north-west of Hobart. The track leads off south from the highway and is well signposted. The track is well constructed, however the rugged and strenuous 25km course takes at least a day to cover. Ensure vehicles are secure, with no valuable items left inside, at the track car park.

Camping and Supplies

There are several campsites spaced regularly along the track for overnight stops. There are also two huts. The first, Vera hut, is situated just over halfway along the track, by Lake Vera. It is also only a few kms from the climbing areas of Sharlands Peak, Burran Pass, White Needle and Philpspeak. The Tahune hut is located near

TASMANIA - FRENCHMAN'S CAP

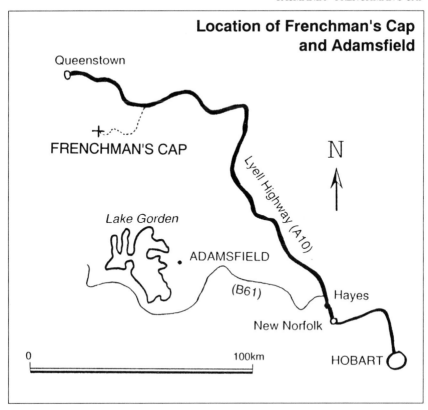

the end of the track at the base of Frenchman's Cap peak. To avoid weighting your already heavy pack of climbing gear with a tent, the huts are a good accommodation option.

All food and fuel supplies should be acquired at the larger, cheaper towns of Hobart and New Norfolk or, if arriving from the north, Queenstown.

Climate and when to go

In winter it is cold and it snows, however some keen alpinists remain undeterred. Being on the west coast, the Frenchman's Cap receives some of Tasmania's more extreme weather: the prevailing wind of the roaring forties and plenty of rain throughout the year. However there is a time of year when the weather is more settled with milder temperatures, although the little shaded south face remains cool. This period is from late Feb through to May, and is the best time to go climbing. Having said that, the weather is changeable. Be prepared for anything, as it has been known to snow at any time.

39

What to take

An extensive rack of equipment including 2 x 50m ropes for climbing all types of adventure routes and setting up belays. Don't forget prusik loops in case you need to back off. Plenty of warm clothing including thermals, hat, gloves, waterproof outers/trousers and jacket are essential, as is a good-sized day pack for taking extra clothes, food and drink on the routes. Head torches are also a good idea in case you get benighted. Helmets are strongly recommended whilst climbing at the Frenchman's Cap.

Recommended classics

Tierry le Fronde	147m	16	(Frenchman's Cap) (Tahune north face)
La Grande Pump	60m	21	(Frenchman's Cap) (NW wall)
The Chimes of Freedom	270m	17	(South-east face)
The Sydney Route	380m	17	(South-east face)
The De Gaulle's Nose Route	330m	23	(South-east face)
The Great Flake	370m	22	(East face)

Author's Rating ***

Guide to climbs

For more information on climbing at the Frenchman's Cap contact the Climbers Club of Tasmania at the University of Tasmania Sport and Recreation Centre, Hobart, Tasmania 7000 Tel: (002) 20 2084.

ADAMSFIELD

SPORT

One of Tasmania's best sport climbing areas is made up by the boulders of Adamsfield on the eastern shore of the tranquil Lake Gordon in classically rugged Tasmania country. Adamsfield is about 2 hours' drive west of Hobart, turning off the Lyell highway (A10) after Hayes onto the B61. The rocks are about ½ hour's walk from the car park. The conglomerate boulders are of good quality, housing about 30 climbs, mainly steep and overhanging 10-20m in length, bolt protected with grades 18-26. This area is being nicely developed with heaps of potential remaining. For more information contact CCT Hobart.

FEDERATION PEAK

This massive quartzite spire is hidden deep in the wild and remote south-west of Tasmania. Australia's longest climb of 800m can be found here, as can other established middle grade routes of around 600m, and a bushwalker's track to the top with some outrageous exposure of 500m at one point! However be warned, Federation Peak is rarely climbed upon. A walk of at least two days is required to reach the base of this very isolated mountain. The climbing is serious adventure style and alpine in nature with loose rock and large runouts all being part of the fun. In addition the weather is notoriously bad. Federation Peak is definitely a place for the experienced only, where summer climbing is the only option. Reasonable camping with no facilities is possible quite close to the rock. There is infinite potential for long adventure climbs at Federation Peak, as most of the rock around the few established routes remains unclimbed. For more information about climbing at Federation Peak contact the Climbers Club of Tasmania or the Tasmanian University Climbing Club.

MOUNT WELLINGTON (THE ORGAN PIPES)

Mount Wellington is conveniently positioned standing 1200m over Hobart. The 100m columnar formation has excellent multi-pitch crack climbs and gives nice exposure with fantastic views over the city and across the sea.

Geology: Dolerite

Number of climbs: 300

Grade of climbs: 10-25

Potential for new routes: Yes, if you bolt them

Rock quality: Sound

Protection: Few bolted routes, mostly natural pro

Length of climbs: 15-100m, few single, mostly multi-pitch

Predominant climbing style: Long cracks

SPORT

Location and Access
Mount Wellington is located just a short drive from the city of Hobart. Exit the city south via the Huon Highway. After 8km turn right at Fern Tree. The winding road will take you to the car park at the top of the mountain. The cliff is 15 minutes' walk from here. There is no camping in the park.

Climate and when to go
The summer and autumn (Nov-May) are the seasons for climbing Mount Wellington, Feb & Mar being best. On colder days it might be suitable to climb in the morning sun, as the cliff faces east.

Tim Chappell on Punk (19), The Organ Pipes, Tasmania.
Photo: Kate Chappell

What to take

In your rack of natural protection, take some big gear. Large hexes and friends are a necessity on some pitches.

Location of Mount Wellington, Mount Brown and The Totem Pole

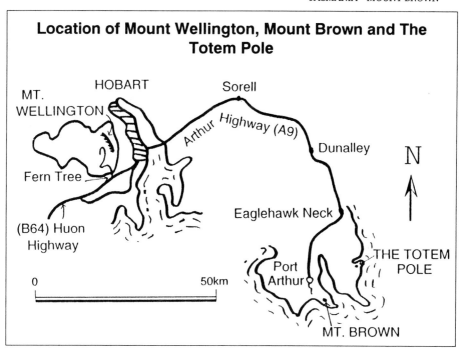

Author's rating **

Guide to climbs
Guidebook available from one of the adventure shops in the city.

MOUNT BROWN

Mount Brown is one of Tasmania's newest and most exciting sport climbing crags. Described as 'awesome', the compact dolorite sea cliffs of the Tasman Peninsula hold steep and inspiring routes in a very atmospheric location.

> **Geology:** Dolorite
>
> **Number of climbs:** 40
>
> **Grade of climbs:** 15-25 (Middle grades)
>
> **Potential for new routes:** Yes (bolted)
>
> **Rock quality:** Excellent
>
> **Protection:** Bolts, SLCDs
>
> **Length of climbs:** 10-35m single pitch
>
> **Predominant climbing style:** Overhang, face
>
> **SPORT**

Location and Access

Mount Brown is located on the Tasman Peninsula in the south-east of Tasmania, 100km from Hobart. Head east from Hobart on the Arthur Highway (A9). Follow this for 100km through Sorell, Dunalley and across the Eaglehawk Neck onto the peninsula down to the town of Port Arthur. Take a 5 minute drive south on a small road from Port Arthur to park at the Remarkable Cave car park. A 40 minute walk east from here will find Mount Brown. (Ask for Mount Brown or the Paradisico Cliffs.)

Camping and Supplies

Camping is available at the Gordon Point Caravan Park located a couple of kms before Port Arthur. Supplies are best sought at Hobart or Sorell before arriving at Port Arthur, as there are no banks and shopping can be expensive on the Peninsula.

Climate and when to go

Three season climbing from spring through to autumn (Sept-May) is possible as Mount Brown is on the more sheltered eastern side of this weathered island. Conditions in winter can be quite gruesome.

What to take

The climbs at Mount Brown are either bolted throughout or a mixture of bolts and the odd friend placement. Quickdraws and a set of SLCDs (including small ones) will do the job here.

Useful information

For more information about climbing at Mount Brown contact the Climbers Club of Tasmania, Hobart.

THE TOTEM POLE

Some extraordinary climbing is possible on one of Tasmania's most distinctive coastal features. The dramatic free standing pinnacle named The Totem Pole is located on the east coast of the Tasman Peninsula somewhere round Cape Hauy. For information about climbing this unique pillar contact the Climbers Club of Tasmania in Hobart.

FREYCINET PENINSULA NATIONAL PARK/
THE HAZARDS, MOUNT AMOS

Geology: Granite

Number of climbs: 400

Grade of climbs: 10-28 mostly middle grade

Potential for new routes: Yes

Rock quality: Sound

Protection: Some bolts, mainly natural pro

Length of climbs: 10-250m single and lots of multi-pitch

Predominant climbing style: Slab, sea cliffs

Location and Acces

The Freycinet Peninsula is located about 180km south-east of Launceston. Take

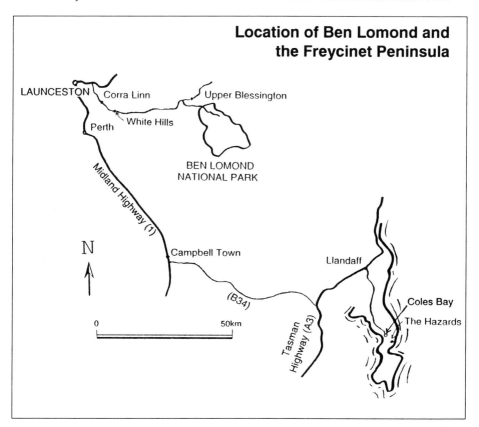

45

the B41 south to Perth to connect with the Midland Highway. After about 70km just after Campbelltown, turn left onto road B34. Follow this road for 60km, then turn left onto the Tasman Highway. At the town of Llandaff, turn right for the road down to the National Park. The Hazards are situated just a few kms south of the holiday town Codes Bay on the eastern side of Peninsula.

Camping and Supplies
Camping is permitted within the National Park. Water however is not available. You would be best advised to stock up in Launceston or a bigger town like Bichena rather than rely on the small and rather expensive town of Coles Bay.

Climate and when to go
Being on the Eastern coast and at sea level, The Hazards can be quite sheltered from Tasmania's prevailing wind and weather front, making climbing possible all year round.

What to take
Plenty of natural gear plus 2 x 50m ropes. Drinking water.

Author's rating *

Guide to climbs

For more information on climbing at The Hazards contact the Climbers Club of Tasmania at Launceston College Climbing Gym, Brisbane St, Launceston, Tas 7250. Access through Allgoods Pty Ltd, 71 York St, Launceston, Tas 7250. Tel (003) 31 3644.

BEN LOMOND NATIONAL PARK

The Ben Lomond cliffs are more superbly positioned columnar outcrops high on the mountain of Legges Tor. The soaring vertical cracks are a dream for the technical jammer. For the most part it is crack climbing in its purest form.

Geology: Dolorite
Number of climbs: 200
Grade of climbs: 18-22
Potential for new routes: No
Rock quality: Good
Protection: Natural pro
Length of climbs: 20-100m multi-pitch
Predominant climbing style: Vertical cracks

Location and Access
The Ben Lomond NP is located 60km east of Launceston, about an hour's drive. Exit the city east via the Tasman Highway (A3). After a few km take the first right turning. Pass through Corralinn and White Hills. Stay on this road for 45km. Just before the town of Upper Blessington, turn right following the sign to Ben Lomond National Park. The cliffs vary from 20 to 45 minute's walk from the car park.

Camping and Supplies
Camping is available within the national park. Supplies are best bought at Launceston, although there is an alpine village shop in the park.

Climate and when to go
As the cliffs are situated at 1000m+, this is definitely a summer climbing venue (Nov-Mar).

Author's rating *

Guide to climbs: As before.

CATARACT GORGE
Geology: Dolorite

Number of climbs: 250

Grade of climbs: 14-25

Potential for new routes: No

Rock quality: Good

Protection: Bolts and natural pro

Length of climbs: 15-25m single pitch

Predominant climbing style: Face and cracks

SPORT

Location and Access
The gorge is 10 minutes' walk from Launceston city centre. Head south-west on Paterson Street. This crosses over the end of the gorge where the south Esk river meets the Tamar river. Walking tracks to the climbing lead from here.

Camping and Supplies
There is no camping in the gorge.

Guide to climbs
For information on climbing in the gorge, try The Wilderness Shop, 174 Charles Street; Paddy Pallin, 59 Brisbane Street; or Allgoods, 60 Elizabeth Street.

SISTERS BEACH

Geology: Quartzite

Number of climbs: 50

Grade of climbs: 15-27

Potential for new routes: No

Rock quality: Sound

Protection: Bolts

Length of climbs: 10-25m

Predominant climbing style: Face, overhangs

SPORT

Location and Access
Sisters Beach is located in the Rocky Cape National Park, 200km north-west of Launceston on the beautiful Tasmanian coast. Leave Launceston by the Bass Highway. Stay on this road for almost all the journey, passing through Deloraine, Ulverstone and Burnie, until the small town of Boat Harbour is reached. Turn right here to enter the park and find Sisters Beach.

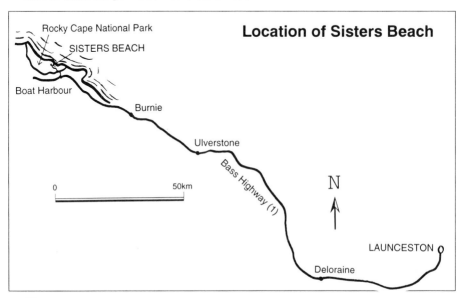

Camping and Supplies

Camping is allowed within the park and facilities include toilets and water. Buy supplies from Burnie and Ulverstone rather than the village at Sisters Beach.

Climate and when to go

Being on the northern coast, Sisters Beach is relatively sheltered from Tasmania's notorious weather, making year round climbing a real possibility.

What to take

10 or so quickdraws and a few slings will suffice here.

Guide to climbs:

For more information on climbing at Sisters Beach, as before.

Useful addresses

Launceston College Climbing Gym
Brisbane Street, Launceston, Tas 7250
Access through: Allgoods Pty Ltd
71 York Street, Launceston, Tas 7250
Tel (03) 31 3644

University of Tasmania (climbing gym)
Sport and Recreation Centre
Hobart, Tas 7000
Tel (02) 20 2084

The Tasmanian Travel Centre
corner of St John and Paterson Street
Tel (03) 37 3111

Paddy Pallin (equipment)
59 Brisbane Street
Launceston, Tas

The Tasmanian Travel Centre
80 Elizabeth Street
Hobart
Tel (002) 30 0250

Department of Environment & Land Management
134 MacQuarrie Street (PO Box 44A, Tas, 7001)
Hobart, Tas 7000
Tel (002) 31 0777 Fax (002) 240 884

Tasmanian Department of Tourism, Sport and Recreation
149 King Street
Sydney, NSW 2000

The Wilderness Shop (equipment)
174 Charles Street
Launceston, Tas

Allgoods (equipment)
60 Elizabeth Street
Launceston, Tas

Paddy Pallin (equipment)
76 Elizabeth Street
Hobart
Tel (002) 31 0777

The Wilderness Shop (equipment)
The Galleria, Salamanca Place
Hobart
Head Office Tel (002) 34 9366

SOUTH AUSTRALIA

A climbing trip to South Australia would have to include the sparse and rugged land of the Flinders Ranges; Pleasant gorges lead the way to the prize of Moonarie. There are also some great day trips from Adelaide, to break up the journey.

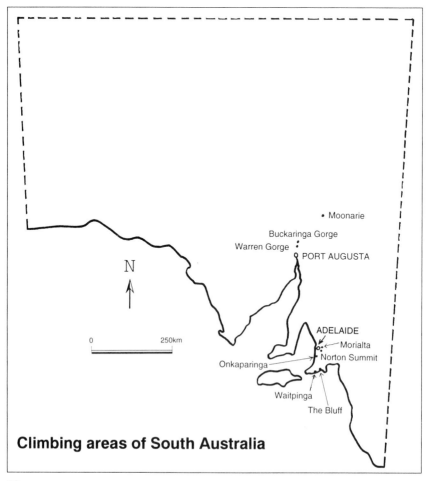

Climbing areas of South Australia

MOONARIE

This is without question South Australia's best climbing venue, such is the grandeur of its setting high on the crater rim of Wilpena Pound. The views at this remote location are quite incredibly panoramic. The land stretches away over the rippling ranges to meet distant clusters of mountains which gently sculpt the horizon. The hike to the cliff is worthy in itself, without mentioning the fantastic walls, corners, buttresses, cracks and faces you are confronted with on arrival. All styles of climbing are catered for, though the more experienced are best suited at Moonarie as climbs are typically exposed and sustained on natural protection.

This wild climbing area, with little sign of human impact, is not for everyone. But for those who enjoy camping on the mountainside and have a few days to spare, Moonarie will be a very special place.

Geology: Quartzite sandstone

Number of climbs: 400+

Grade of climbs: 4-28

Potential for new routes: Yes

Rock quality: Good

Protection: Some bolts, 90% natural pro

Length of climbs: 10-144m single and multi-pitch

Predominant climbing style: All styles except slab

Location and Access

Moonarie is located in the Flinders Ranges National Park 450km north of Adelaide. Take the Princess Highway from Adelaide heading north for 300km towards Port Augusta. 7km before Port Augusta turn right onto Highway 47, signposted Quorn, Hawker, the Flinders Ranges. Pass through Quorn, then at Hawker turn right through the town to the National Park and Wilpena. 40km from Hawker turn left at the signposted Arkaroo Rock. After about a kilometre turn left onto a gravel track. Follow this for 150m. After the road takes a long right bend, follow the dirt track branching to the right across the mud and grass to find the bottom campsite and car park in the trees. (Take great care in driving from the road to the campsite as the track takes a little improvising at times, due to rain damage!) The crag is about 45 minutes' walk from here, the last part being steep. Go down over the creek, then cross the fence. The track is marked by intermittent piles of rocks (cairns) and will take you to the base of the cliffs by the southern descent gully. The small rock plateau of top camp is also here.

Camping and Supplies

There are two options for camping at Moonarie. Firstly, base camp; there are no facilities here and a 45 minute hike to the crag is required. It does offer the shelter of the trees in the event of a storm. Alternatively, there is the top camp, a small rock plateau with room for two good sized tents at the end of the approach track below the cliffs. This is marked by a dustbin, a 'steep climb' road sign and breathtaking views! Although the more arduous option of the two, for a prolonged stay you will be well rewarded for dragging camping equipment and a few days' food here, for what is surely an

Location of Moonarie, Warren Gorge and Buckaringa Gorge

FLINDERS RANGES
NATIONAL PARK

N

WILPENA

MOONARIE

0   50km

HAWKER

BUCKARINGE
GORGE

WARREN
GORGE

(47)

QUORN

PORT AUGUSTA

STIRING
NORTH

ADELAIDE
300km

Princess
Highway (1)

enriching experience. There is also a well constructed rainwater tank a short distance up the descent gully (enquire with the ranger on the present water level).

For food and fuel the larger supermarkets of Port Augusta are best. This is also the last town with 24 hour petrol. A further 15km into the park is Wilpena, where laundry, hot showers, toilet, restaurant/bar and a small expensive mini-mart and petrol station can be found.

There is a total fire ban 1st Nov-30th Apr.

Climbing areas of Moonarie

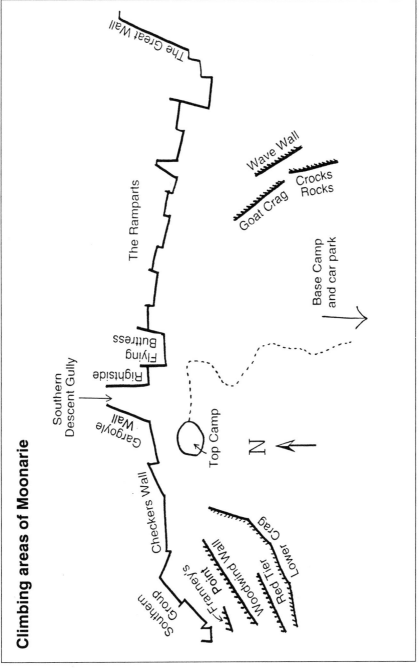

Climate and when to go

The season at Moonarie reaches both ends of the weather scale. Winter (Jun-Aug) is cold and summer (Dec-Feb) is hot, reaching into the 40s°C, making spring and autumn the best time to climb. There is also the occasional thunderstorm with continual downpours for up to two days. In this event retreat may be a good choice to avoid vehicles being bogged.

What to take

A full rack of SLCD and wires. Big hexes and friends would also be of use on some routes. Drinking water for base camp. A shovel for dealing with human waste and paper.

Recommended classics

The Flying Buttress	15	105m	(Flying Buttress)
Pagoda	17	100m	(Checker's Wall)
Casablanca	19	100m	(Checker's Wall)
The Prince	19	33m	(Gargoyle Wall)
Expiry Date	22	55m	(The Ramparts)
Sweeping Statement	24	55m	(The Ramparts)
Miles from Nowhere	18	100m	(The Ramparts)
The Endless Pitch	23	50m	(The Ramparts)
Downwind of Angels	19	55m	(The Great Wall)
Robin Hood	24	50m	(The Great Wall)
No Muesli Required	19	15m	(Woodwind Wall)

Useful information

A stretcher can be found in a small crevice by top camp.

Please notify the National Park of all climbing trips on (086) 48 0048 or (086) 48 4244. In case of emergency ring the NPWS duty ranger on (086) 48 4248. Ask to use the phone at the Prelinna Homestead on the main road just before the Arkaroo Rock turn off.

Author's rating ***

Guide to climbs

Moonarie, a Rock Climber's Guide edited by Tony Parker (1993)

The following areas make excellent locations for an afternoon's climbing and overnight stops to break the long journey to Moonarie.

WARREN GORGE

Geology: Sandstone
Number of climbs: 7
Grade of climbs: 16-22
Potential for new routes: No
Rock quality: sound
Protection: Bolts, natural pro required for anchors
Length of climbs: 15m single pitch
Predominant climbing style: Face

Location and Access (see map p52)

Warren Gorge is situated 350km north of Adelaide in the Flinders Range. From Adelaide keep to the Princess Highway for 300km until the town of Stirling North, just before Port Augusta is reached. Turn right here after 40km to the small town of Quorn. Turn left onto a dirt road here. Turn left again in 10km for Warren Gorge. The climbs are on the right-hand side, on a smooth face perpendicular to the road. Look closely to see the fixed hangers as they are camouflaged with paint.

Camping and Supplies

Camping is allowed within the gorge. There is a site with no facilities just below the climbs. Supplies are available at Quorn, but Port Augusta would be a better choice.

Climate and when to go

Spring (Sept-Nov) and autumn (Feb-May) are the best times to visit Warren Gorge, although summer could be a possibility, the gorge being in the shade after the morning sun.

Useful numbers:

In an emergency ring the NPWS duty ranger on (086) 48 4248 at Quorn.

Guide to climbs:

No guide available.

BUCKARINGA GORGE

Geology: Sandstone

Number of climbs: 50

Grade of climbs: 16-25

Potential for new routes: No

Rock quality: Sound

Protection: Natural Pro

Length of climbs: 25m single pitch

Predominant climbing style: Face

Location and Access (see map P52)

Follow directions to Quorn (see Warren Gorge) and take the left dirt road from there. Stay on the road for 15km to find the left turn to Buckaringa Gorge. The climbing is on the long wall of columnar appearance directly in front of the road leading to the gorge.

Climate and when to go

Spring (Sept-Nov) and autumn (Feb-May) are the best times to visit Buckaringa Gorge.

Useful numbers

In case of emergency ring the NPWS duty ranger on (086) 48 4248 at Quorn.

Guide to climbs

Not available as yet.

DEVIL'S PEAK

Located close to Quorn, this area has recently received much attention from South Australian climbers, with the first ascent of many new routes. Devil's Peak is fast becoming one of SA's most popular crags. For more information contact the Climbing Club of South Australia, PO Box 130, Magill, SA 5072 or one of the equipment shops listed at the back of this section.

If you are in Adelaide for any length of time, there are some nice crags awaiting your visit. All are easy day trips from the city.

MORIALTA

Geology: Sandstone

Number of climbs: 320

Grade of climbs: 4-25 (easy to middle)

Potential for new routes: No

Rock quality: Fair

Protection: Few bolts, mostly natural pro or top roping

Length of climbs: 5-35m single pitch, few 2 pitch

Predominant climbing style: All styles

Location and Access

Morialta Conservation Park is located 15km east of the city in the scenic Adelaide hills. Exit the city to the east via the North Terrace. After a short distance branch right onto Magill Road. Follow this road for about 10km to the end. Turn left here onto the new Norton Summit Road. Do not enter the park through the main entrance at the bottom of the road. Park in the lay-by on the right-hand side 5.3km from the junction, up the winding road. To gain access to the Morialta cliffs, go through the gate on the left-hand side of the road and follow a series of tracks down to the base of the cliffs.

On Sundays and public holidays, climbing has been banned below the first and second waterfalls.

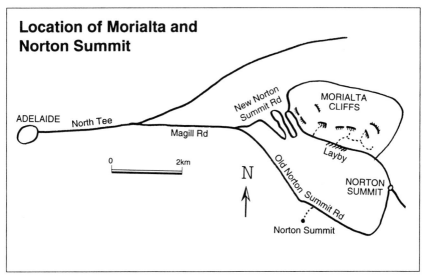

Camping and Supplies
Camping is not allowed within the park.

Climate and when to go
The cliffs at Morialta are spread around the park at all angles to the sun, making climbing possible at all times of the year with milder temperatures in autumn and spring. Summers are typically hot and dry and winters are colder (average 15°C) with more rainfall.

What to take
A basic rack of wires and friends along with a single rope will do the trick. A climbing helmet is also a wise precaution for belayers as loose rock is not unheard of!

Guide to climbs
Rock Climbs Around Adelaide edited by Nyrie Dodd.

NORTON SUMMIT

Geology: Sandstone

Number of climbs: 25

Grade of climbs: 3-29 (most are short and hard)

Potential for new routes: No

Rock quality: Sound

Protection: Mostly pure sport climbs, few traditional climbs

Length of climbs: 10-80m most single, few multi-pitch

Predominant climbing style: Overhang/roof

SPORT

Location and Access (see map p57)
Follow directions for Morialta to the end of Magill Road. Turn right here along the old Norton Summit Road. The cliffs and caves are on the right-hand side of the road up a steep embankment. There is a right lay-by to park in after about 4km, well before the sharp left bend up to Norton Summit town. A very steep and loose (tread carefully) track leads up to the climbing from here.

Camping and Supplies
There is no camping at Norton Summit.

Climate and when to go
Year round climbing is possible at Norton Summit, particularly in the cave which remains sheltered from sun and rain.

What to take
Hard overhanging climbs are Norton Summit's speciality, which are bolted top to bottom. If you want to climb hard then quickdraws and a rope are fine.

Guide to climbs
Rock Climbs Around Adelaide edited by Nyrie Dodd.

THE BLUFF

Geology: Granite
Number of climbs: 50
Grade of climbs: 6-24 (easy, middle)
Potential for new routes: No
Rock quality: Fair
Protection: Few bolts, mostly natural pro
Length of climbs: 2-42m single, some 2 pitch
Predominant climbing style: Slab (sand cliffs)

Location and Access (see map p60)
The Bluff, which is also known as Rosetta Head, is located 80km south of Adelaide on the south-eastern coast of the Fleurieu Peninsula. Pick your route from Adelaide via minor roads to the southern town of Victor Harbour. Exit this town on the Yankalilla Road to the west. After 1km take the left fork to Waitpinga. Turn left near the hospital back to the sea front. This leads down to The Bluff. For popular areas of Penny Lane, the slabs and Bandaid Wall park by the jetty. The Pleasure Dome and Petrol Rock are found further round to the southern end of the bluff a few hundred metres from the jetty.

Camping and Supplies
There is no camping at The Bluff.

Climate and when to go
This follows the same pattern as for other areas around Adelaide. It should be noted that because The Bluff is a headland on the coast, it can be quite windswept, making a calm day a better choice.

What to take

A standard rack of wires and friends. A single rope.

Guide to climbs

As above.

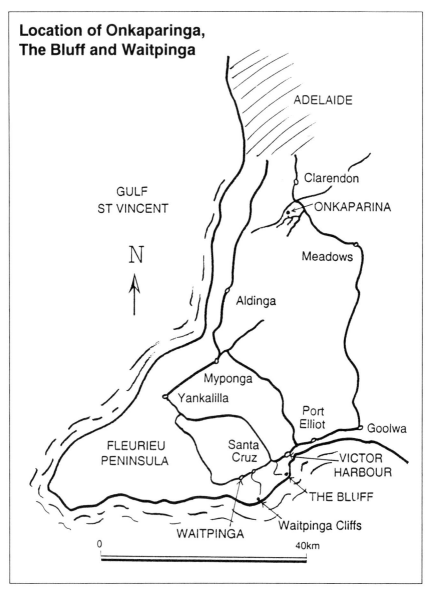

Location of Onkaparinga, The Bluff and Waitpinga

ADELAIDE

Clarendon

GULF
ST VINCENT

ONKAPARINA

N

Meadows

Aldinga

Myponga

Yankalilla

Port
Elliot

Goolwa

FLEURIEU
PENINSULA

Santa
Cruz

VICTOR
HARBOUR

THE BLUFF

Waitpinga Cliffs

WAITPINGA

0   40km

WAITPINGA

Geology: Flaky granite
Number of climbs: 26
Grade of climbs: 4-8 (easy/middle)
Potential for new routes: No
Rock quality: Fair
Protection: Natural pro
Length of climbs: 12-100m single and multi-pitch
Predominant climbing style: Slab

Location and Access

The Waitpinga Cliffs are 90km south of Adelaide on the south-western coast of the Fleurieu Peninsula. To reach the cliffs, take the westerly road to Yankalilla from Victor Harbour. After 1km take a left fork to Waitpinga. A short distance along this road is the small town of Santa Cruz. Turn left here for a few kms' drive down to the cliffs.

The climbing is partly on the Newland Head Conservation Park and partly on private properties. The land is owned by the Carmichaels. Permission to climb must be gained prior to arrival. Tel (085) 52 3267 or Bernie Carmichael (085) 52 3799.

Access to the cliffs is via two descent gullies at either end.

Camping and Supplies

There is no camping at the Waitpinga Cliffs.

Climate and when to go

As for other areas around Adelaide. Avoid the Waitpinga Cliffs at high tide, as big waves make belaying from the lower ledge a treacherous affair.

What to take

Standard rack of wires and camming devices.

Guide to climbs

As before.

ONKAPARINGA

Geology: Sandstone
Number of climbs: 60
Grade of climbs: 6-21 (easy/middle)
Potential for new routes: No
Rock quality: Sound
Protection: Some bolts, natural pro

Length of climbs: 5-30m single pitch

Predominant climbing style: All styles

Location and Access (see map p60)

The Onkaparinga Cliffs are 25km south of Adelaide on the banks of the Onkaparinga river. Take the south road from Adelaide turning off for Clarendon. After Clarendon, about 1½km past the Onkaparinga bridge, turn right to Blewitt Springs. In a few km take the right fork to Chapel Hill Road. Turn right at the next junction, staying on Chapel Hill Road. Park 500m from here in the area on the right. A short walk following the fence line to the gorge leads to the climbing.

Climate and when to go

As for other areas around Adelaide.

Guide to climbs

As before.

Useful addresses

The South Australian Government
Travel Centre
18 King William Street
Adelaide, SA
Tel (08) 212 1505 or
freephone 008 882 092

The National Parks Office
55 Grenfell Street
Adelaide, SA
Tel (08) 216 7777

Climbing Club of South Australia
PO Box 130
Magill SA 5072

Mountain Designs (equipment)
121 Grenfell Street
Adelaide
Tel (08) 232 0696

Annapurna (equipment)
210 Rundle Street
Adelaide
Tel (08) 223 4633

Paddy Pallin (equipment)
228 Rundle Street
Adelaide
Tel (08) 232 5000
freephone 008 80 1119

South Australian Travel Centre
Mezzanine Level
247 Pitt Street
Sydney
NSW 2000
Tel (02) 264 3375

Adelaide Rock Climbing Gym
560 North East Rd
Holden Hill
SA 5088
Tel (08) 266 4090 Fax (08) 266 4091

There is also a climbing wall in the city on West Tce.

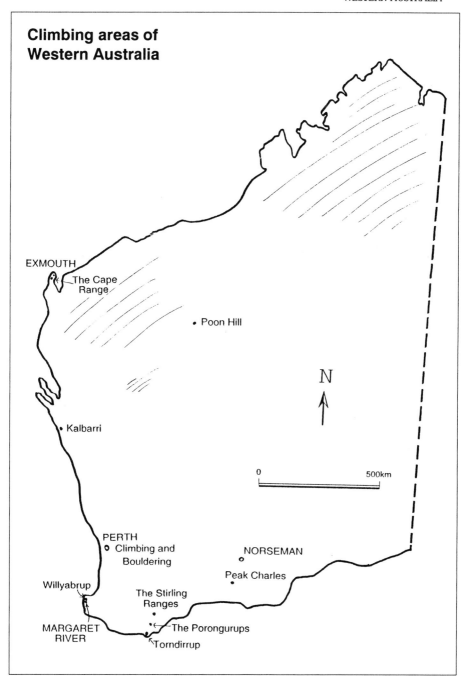

**Climbing areas of
Western Australia**

EXMOUTH
The Cape
Range

• Poon Hill

N
↑

• Kalbarri

0   500km

PERTH
○ Climbing and
Bouldering

NORSEMAN
○

Peak Charles
•

Willyabrup

The Stirling
Ranges
•

MARGARET
RIVER
Torndirrup

The Porongurups

WESTERN AUSTRALIA

Making up almost a third of Australia's land mass, yet giving residence to only 10% of the population, Western Australia is a place to get away from it all. The extensive coast line holds many hidden delights. A climbing tour through Western Australia is an uplifting experience, combining excellent climbing with unspoilt beauty. If you don't fly to Perth, then getting to WA will involve the rather lengthy journey across the Nullabar Plains from the east. This is an experience in itself: hundreds of kilometres of straight road as far as the eye can see, in front and behind. Mind you, there are no rocks or hills, not even a tree to hang off! A fingerboard on the back of your camper van will help sustain a little strength during the transition from east to west!

PEAK CHARLES

If you travel to WA from the east, then the imposing, yet largely undeveloped granite dome of Peak Charles is the first climbing area you will come to. The mass of orange granite specialises in longer adventure type slab climbs and serves as an excellent introduction to WA climbing.

Geology: Granite

Number of climbs: 50

Grade of climbs: 10-20

Potential for new routes: Yes

Rock quality: Good

Protection: Natural pro and some bolts

Length of climbs 20-310m single, mostly multi-pitch

Predominant climbing style: Slab and crack multi-pitch

Location and Access

Peak Charles is about 550km east and south of Perth in the south-west corner of Australia. From the town of Norseman on the end of the Eyre Highway, drive towards Esperance on the highway for 55km. Turn right at the Peak Charles signpost onto a dirt road. Continue a further 40km, taking the left fork at 25km (signposted) to reach the base of the cliffs. There is a campsite at the base and the climbs start on the main cliff a few minutes' walk from here.

The author chalks up on Remnant (22), Moonaire *Photo Stephen Saunders*
The Glasshouse Mountains, Queensland *Photo Alastair Lee*

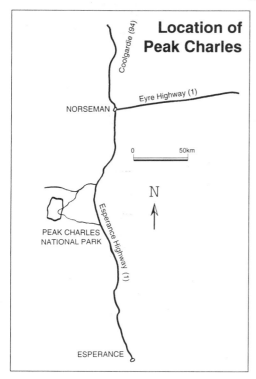

Location of Peak Charles

Camping and Supplies

There is a good camping site at the base of Peak Charles. Unfortunately there is no water supply, so it is necessary to bring your own in.

Food and fuel is readily available from the selection of super- markets and petrol stations in Norseman.

Climate and when to go

Climbing is possible all year round at Peak Charles. Summer (Dec- Feb) is very warm and winter (Jun-Sept) quite cold, but neither are too extreme. Annual rainfall is relatively low, the heaviest downpours arriving in late autumn and winter.

What to take

A good rack of nuts and plenty of friends. You can get away with a single 50m rope, as most of the longer routes finish on the summit, where descent is possible down the left ridge (as seen from the campsite).

Recommended Classics

Guano	170m	18	(Main Cliff)
Trout Dentures	280m	16	(Main Cliff)
Spartacus	100m	17	(Spartacus Slab)

Useful information

For more information on climbing in the Peak Charles National Park contact the Department of Conservation and Land Management in Esperance on (09) 71 3733.

Author's rating *

Guide to climbs

For all climbing areas around Perth *Perth Rock* by Shane Richardson (1996)

Alon Hod leads Robin Hood (24), more classic face climbing on The Great Wall, Moonarie. Photo: Author

THE STIRLING RANGES

The Stirling Ranges are an impressive single row of peaks, which rise abruptly from the surrounding plains. Western Australia's finest adventure climbing is to be found here: long committing lines with astronomical exposure, all in the rich surroundings of WA's beautiful wildlife. A day's cragging in the Stirlings is hard to beat.

Geology: Sandstone conglomerate

Number of climbs: 150

Grade of climbs: 4-21 (easy/middle)

Potential for new routes: Yes

Rock quality: Sound

Protection: Natural pro

Length of climbs: 10-350 single, mostly multi-pitch

Predominant climbing style: Crack, chimney, face, serious adventure leading

Location and Access

The Stirling Range National Park is about 300km south-east of Perth. From Perth exit the city via the Albany Highway (30). After 290km the town of Cranbrook is reached. Turn left here, heading east on North Stirling Road. 60km along will take you to Chester Pass Road. Turn right onto this to enter the National Park.

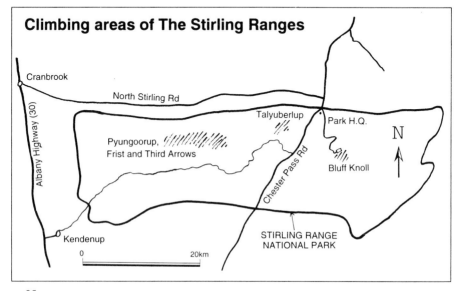

Climbing areas of The Stirling Ranges

Cranbrook

North Stirling Rd

Albany Highway (30)

Pyungoorup, Frist and Third Arrows

Talyuberlup

Park H.Q.

Chester Pass Rd

Bluff Knoll

N

Kendenup

0   20km

STIRLING RANGE
NATIONAL PARK

If arriving from the east, 300km along the south coast highway (2) from Esperance is the town of Jerramungup. Continue straight on here (west) for 65km through Ongerup, then turn left to Borden. Pass through Borden then after about 7km turn right to join the Chester Pass Road. Another 30km will find the National Park.

One of the major climbing areas of the Stirling Ranges is Bluff Knoll (it's also the highest peak at 1073m). The left turning is signposted from Chester Pass Road. The various climbing areas of Bluff Knoll are about an hour's walk from the car park. Other popular areas include Talyuberlup and the First and Third Arrows. These are accessed by fire trails leading from (Pyungoorup) Stirling Range Drive (the right turn from Chester Pass Road). Walking times vary from 45 minutes (Talyuberlup) to 3 hours (Third Arrow and Pyungoorup).

Camping and Supplies

Camping is permitted within the National Park at the Toolbrunup campsite whose facilities are limited. The park headquarters can also be found here. Food and fuel are cheapest from the larger towns of Esperance or Perth. There are good road houses selling petrol and food along the way, including Jerramungup and Cranbrook.

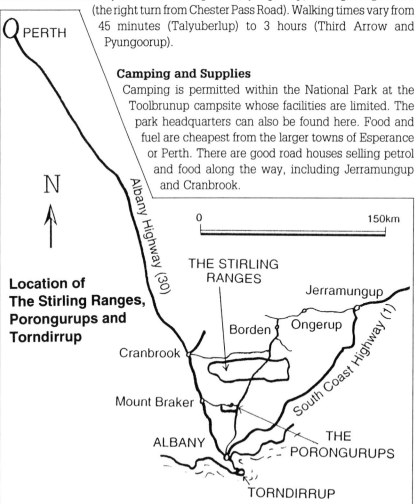

67

Climate and when to go

Spring (Sept-Nov) and autumn (Feb-May) are the best times for climbing in the Stirlings. Summer can be very hot, and it can snow in winter.

What to take

A good rack of wires and friends. 1 x 50m rope (depending on size of party) as easy walks or scrambles are the means of descent.

Recommended Classics

Lincolnshire Poacher	100m	16	(Coyanarup/Sphinx Buttress)
Hellfire Gully	254m	14	(Bluff Knoll, north face)
Capital Seizure	320m	19	(Bluff Knoll, north face)
Jetstream	60m	17	(Bluff Knoll, Bastion Buttress)

Useful information

Climbers are requested to let one of the rangers know of your intentions. Climbers must also register in one of the log books either at the park headquarters (Toolbrunup campsite) or at the assistant ranger's residence by the Bluff Knoll turn off.

Ranger (098) 279 230   Assistant ranger (098) 279 278

There is also rescue equipment at the ranger's office.

For more information on the Stirling Ranges National Park contact SRNP Chester Pass Road, C/O Amelup via Borden, WA 6338.

Author's rating **

Guide to climbs

As before.

PORONGURUPS

The granite domes and outcrops of the Porongurups National Park hold a handful of classics: from short technical faces to lengthier 5 pitch slab outings from the summit of Marmabup Rock (670m). The panorama extends to the distant Stirling Ranges in the north, down to Albany and the southern ocean, all across the beautiful lands of south-western Australia.

Geology: Granite

Number of climbs: 40

Grade of climbs: 5-22 (easy/middle)

Potential for new routes: No

Rock quality: Fair

Protection: Some bolts, natural gear

Length of climbs: 10-287m single and multi-pitch

Predominant climbing style: Slab/face

Location and Access

The Porongurup are approximately 325km south-east of Perth. 300 or so km down the Albany Highway takes you to Mount Barker. Turn left here onto Porongurup Road. The National Park is 20km on the right. The popular climbing area of Marmabup Rock is accessed via the Wansborough Walk and Devil's Slide tracks. The climbs are on the east face, about 1 hour's walk. Castle Rock is found by turning onto Castle Rock Road from Porongurup Road, walking time 20 minutes. The climbing area of Twin Peaks involves an hour's bush bash from the Millinup track on the south side of the park.

Camping and Supplies

Camping is allowed on the west of Bolganup Road. Contact the ranger, who lives on the left by the park entrance, for details. Mount Barker is nearest for food and fuel.

Climate and when to go

Climbing in the Porongurups is best in spring (Sept-Nov) and autumn (Feb-May), summers getting hot, while winter is a little chilly!

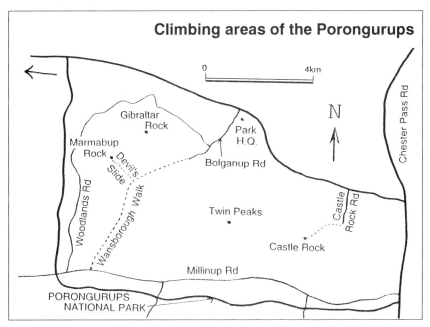

Climbing areas of the Porongurups

What to take
Standard rack of wires and nuts. 2 x 50m ropes are required for some abseils.

Recommended classics

Riddy Was Here	90m	15	(Marmabup Rock)
Meaningless	20m	22	(Castle Rock)

Useful information
For more information on the Porongurups NP contact Porongurup National Park, Bolganup Road, RMB 1112, Mount Barker, WA 6324.

Author's rating *

Guide to climbs
As before.

TORNDIRRUP (ALBANY)

The white/grey granite sea cliffs of the Torndirrup National Park give some of the state's finest natural lines on excellent rock. Located on stunning coastline, it's another great from WA.

Geology: Granite

Number of climbs: 140

Grade of climbs: 4-24 (middle grade)

Potential for new routes: No

Rock quality: Excellent

Protection: Natural pro

Length of climbs: 7-118m mostly single, some multi-pitch

Predominant climbing style: Crack

Location and Access
The Torndirrup National Park is on the peninsula forming the Princess Royal Harbour, 10km south of Albany. To reach the National Park, follow the signs from Albany to The Gap and Whaling Station. After a short drive you will be in the National Park. Climbing areas include The Gap, Natural Bridge, Eastern Amphitheatre (Gap car park) and Peak Head (Stoney Hill Lookout). All are a short walk from the car parks.

Camping and Supplies
There is no camping within the National Park.

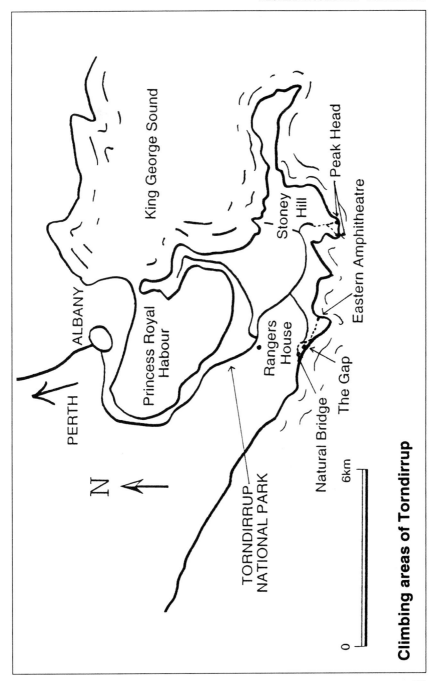

Climbing areas of Torndirrup

Klaus Klein at Bob's Hollow. Photo: Kim Carrigan

Climate and when to go

Three season climbing is possible at Torndirrup Sept-May, although the odd summer's day may be a little hot. Most of the climbs start quite close to sea level, so keep an eye out for freak waves and don't climb when seas are rough.

What to take

Rack of nuts and friends plus 1 x 50m rope. Be prepared for coastal conditions by having wind and waterproof clothing at hand.

Recommended classics

Listen to the Wind Blow	20m	22	(Eastern Amphitheatre)
Atolls Away	25m	24	(Eastern Amphitheatre)
Baylac Direct	100m	18	(Peak Head)

Useful information

For more information on the Torndirrup National Park contact the Albany Tourist Bureau, corner of Peel Place and York Street, Albany, WA. Tel (098) 41 1088.

Author's rating **

Guide to climbs

Same again.

WILLYABRUP (MARGARET RIVER)

This is Western Australia's most developed crag, with lots of single pitch routes of varying styles all situated close to the touristic town of Margaret River looking over the spectacular coast of the Indian Ocean. There are also many other activities on offer: surfing, caving and wine tasting, for example. For a weekend trip from Perth, Willyabrup is a popular choice.

Geology: Granite/limestone mix

Number of climbs: 150

Grade of climbs: 5-25 all grades

Potential for new routes: No

Rock quality: Sound

Protection: Bolts and natural pro

Length of climbs: 10-40m single, some 2 pitch

Predominant climbing style: All styles

SPORT

Location and Access

Willyabrup is located 230km south of Perth on the west coast, in the Leeuwin-Naturaliste National Park. Follow the coastal road south (1), passing through Bunbury at 180km. Continue by the coast leaving the main highway just after Busselton, to find the town of Yallingup. Drive south from here along the Caves

Road. After about 16km turn right on to a dirt track marked Willyabrup Downs, across from the Gralyn Winery. After 2km and three sharp bends, park where the track divides. The crag is a few minutes' walk across the field in front of the sea. The field is not in the National Park. It is owned by the Cullen family. Permission to cross the field must be obtained by phoning (097) 555 277. Please treat their land with respect by keeping to the foot track, which leads to the northern end of the Willyabrup Cliffs.

Camping and Supplies
There is no camping at the crag. The nearest campsite is 5km further south on Caves Road, at the Gracetown turning. The Colray Caravan Park has good facilities including toilets and hot showers. Local towns Margaret River and Yallingup have adequate supplies of food and fuel. Larger towns Busselton or Bunbury are slightly easier on the pocket.

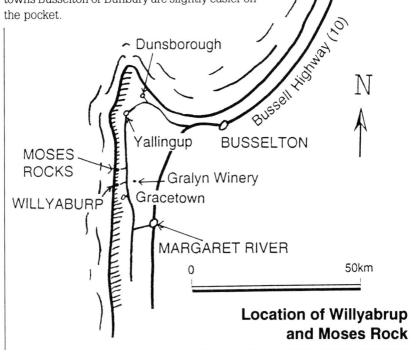

**Location of Willyabrup
and Moses Rock**

Climate and when to go
Climbing is possible at Willyabrup from spring to autumn (Sept-May) while winter on the south-west coast can be quite harsh.

What to take
You don't need the biggest rack in the world to climb at Willyabrup, with a lot of the climbs having some bolts to help you out.

Recommended classics
Corpus Delecti	20m	18	(North Buttress)
Rape and Pillage	40m	23	(Main Buttress)
One for the Road	18m	19	(No 4 Buttress)

Useful information
Tel (097) 555 277 for permission to cross the Cullens' field to access the crag.

Author's rating **

Guide to climbs
You guessed it!

MOSES ROCKS AND SEA CLIFFS
(MARGARET RIVER)

Another great collection of short climbs on the south-west coast. The Moses Rocks area also has good bouldering, nicely complementing the adjacent area of Willyabrup.

Geology: Granite

Number of climbs: 40

Grade of climbs: 10-23

Potential for new routes: No

Rock quality: Good

Protection: Bolts and natural pro

Length of climbs: 6-25 single pitch

Predominant climbing style: Face, crack and bouldering

SPORT

Location and Access
Moses Rocks and sea cliffs are situated at the southern end of the Moses Rock

beach 250km south of Perth in the Leeuwin-Naturaliste National Park. Take the main coastal highway, south from Perth (1). Pass through Bunbury at 180km. Keeping to the coast, leave the main highway after Busselton. Continue a further 20km to take a left inland turn, to the town of Yallingup. From Yallingup, drive south on Caves Road for 15km to turn right onto Moses Rock Road. Follow this for a short distance to find the car park. Walk south for about $^{1}/_{2}$km along the beach to find the boulders and broken sea cliffs.

Camping and Supplies
There is no camping on the Moses Rock Beach.

Climate and when to go
Climbing is possible at Moses Rocks Sept-May (spring, summer and autumn) due to a relatively mild climate for Australia.

What to take
A surfboard?

Guide to climbs
Margaret River by Shane Richardson (1996)

KALBARRI
One of Western Australia's most recently discovered cliffs, Kalbarri is being well developed despite its remote location. At a glance the gorge appears to be friable and of poor quality, however amidst all this there are many compact areas of dream rock. The intrepid route setter will be well rewarded. Climbing is done on smooth red walls and overhangs, just a few of the many features on this spectacular formation. Great sport climbing is the theme in this beautiful place, which is fast becoming WA's most talked about crag.

Geology: Sandstone

Number of climbs: 25

Grade of climbs: 14-26

Potential for new routes: Yes

Rock quality: Good

Protection: Bolts and chains rap, some natural routes

Length of climbs: 10-25m single pitch

Predominant climbing style: Face, overhang

SPORT

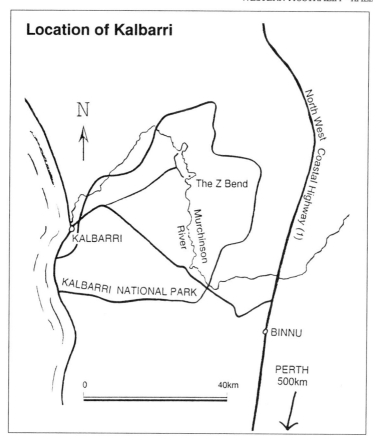

Location of Kalbarri

Location and Access

The gorge is situated in the Kalbarri National Park, some 500km north of Perth (7 hour drive). Exit Perth via the Great Northern Highway. Branch left after 50km to join the Brand Highway (1). Stay on this road for approximately 450km until the well-signposted left turnoff for Kalbarri and the National Park come into view just after the small town of Binnu. The entrance to the National Park is 55km along this road on the right. 20km into the park, is a T junction. Turn right here to the Z bend (not left to the loop). There is a car park and toilets at the end of the road. 15-20 minutes' walk will take you to the climbs via the steep gully. The climbs are about 1km further down the gorge on the left (true).

Camping and Supplies

There is no camping allowed within the National Park. There are however numerous campsites/caravan parks in the nearby town of Kalbarri, where you will also find two supermarkets and a petrol station.

77

Climate and when to go
The best time to climb in Kalbarri is during the cooler months away from summer, when the temperatures are often in excess of 35°C. Feb-Nov has idyllic climbing conditions with the developed side of the gorge being shaded from the sun.

What to take
Although there are some traditional routes where nuts and friends are required, most climbs are bolted with fixed hangers and have rap chains where quickdraws will suffice.
Plenty of water.

Useful information
Climbers must contact the ranger before undertaking a climbing trip.
Tel (099) 37 1146 Fax (099) 37 1437. Rangers must also be consulted before developing a new area as visibility of fixed protection is to be kept to a minimum. For more information contact: The Climbing Association of Western Australia, PO Box 623, Subiaco, WA 6008.

Guide to climb
Contact Mountain Designs to find out the present situation on guidebooks.

CAPE RANGE NATIONAL PARK

A handful of bolted limestone routes awaits those who travel into the tropical climate and semi-desert terrain of the Cape Range. The climbs are hidden behind dusty ranges in the rocky canyons and gorges of this desiccated National Park. Clear days where the sun burns down on the red/brown rock are commonplace, giving pleasant views of the Exmouth Gulf and the offshore coral of the Ningaloo Reef.

Geology: Limestone

Number of climbs: 20

Grade of climbs: 14-26

Potential for new routes: Yes

Rock quality: Sound

Protection: Bolts and natural pro

Length of climbs: 10-30m single pitch

Predominant climbing style: Steep faces

SPORT

Location and Access

The Cape Range National Park is on the western side of the North West Cape near the town of Exmouth, 350km north of the west coast town of Carnarvon. Climbing can be found on both the east and west sides of the park. For the east, turn left onto the Charles Knife Road (signposted). If heading north on the Minilya-Exmouth Road, the turning is approx. 20km before Exmouth. Pull into the right on

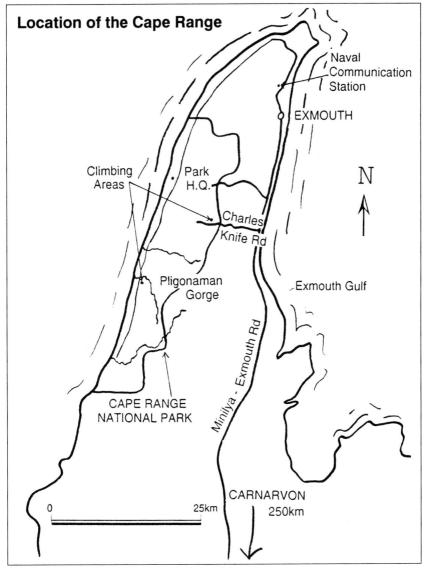

Location of the Cape Range

a gravel area near the edge of the canyon, about 10km along the road, not far from the park entrance. Down and left from the gravel area is the dusty cliff top of the 15m brown escarpment of the canyon. Look for bolts to abseil into the climbs from here. The better climbing in the west of the park is found by following the main road north of Exmouth past the naval communications station, around the head of the cape then down the west coast. 30km into the park is the Pilgonaman Gorge on the left-hand side of the road. The climbs are on the smooth red limestone face on the right side entrance to the gorge, clearly visible from the road. Take the dirt track from the main track of the national park, to park at the end, a couple of minutes' walk from the rock.

Camping and Supplies
Camping is permitted on the western side of the park, where facilities are limited to toilets with no water. Fees are payable. Exmouth office (099) 491676 Fax (099) 491580. Visitor centre in the National Park (099) 492808. On the north-east of the cape is the town of Exmouth, where numerous campsites/caravan parks can be found, as well as a good supermarket and tourist information.

Climate and when to go
On your journey to the Cape Range, a short distance after leaving the main highway, you will cross the Tropic of Capricorn, making this a genuine tropical crag. Winter (May-Sept) has the most comfortable conditions (average 25°C!) and is the best time to climb this far north in Australia. Spring and autumn are possibilities for climbing on days when westerly sea breezes pick up, dropping temperatures by a few degrees. Summer is definitely out of the question. Exerting oneself in temperatures of 35°C+ and scorching sunlight is quite dangerous.

What to take
Plenty of drinking water is essential. There is no water within the National Park. The majority of routes are bolted with chains, so quickdraws will do for those intending only to sport climb.
    A brimmed hat and sunscreen to protect from the sun.

Useful information
Take great care whilst driving around the Cape Range, particularly at dusk, as literally hundreds of kangaroos inhabit the National Park. For more information on the Cape Range contact CRNP, PO Box 201, Exmouth 6707. Tel (099) 49 1676 or (099) 49 1428.

Guide to climbs
Northern Rock by Shane Richardson (1996)

POON HILL/ROUND HILL

Poon Hill is one of Australia's most isolated crags, placed 400km inland to the east of the barren outlay of the Pilbara. For those who venture this far into the outback, Poon Hill's north-eastern escarpment awards many a classic.

Geology: Sandstone

Number of climbs: 40

Grade of climbs: 6-26

Potential for new routes: Yes

Rock quality: Sound

Protection: Bolts and natural pro

Length of climbs: 8-16m single pitch

Predominant climbing style: All styles

SPORT

Location and Access

400km south of the coastal town of Port Headland on the Great Northern Highway is the mining town of Newman. Poon Hill is 10km east of Newman. Exit Newman to the coast along the Great Northern Highway (95), past the airport towards the Capricorn Roadhouse. After 2.5km turn right onto the second of two dirt roads. This track leads up the north-eastern side of Poon Hill. Park on this side of the dry river bed, level with the cliffs. Climbs can be found further west along the precipice. Alternatively Poon Hill can be reached from Perth simply by picking up the Great Northern Highway and staying on it for 1200km!

Camping and Supplies

There is no camping at Poon Hill. Several caravan/camping sites are to be found within

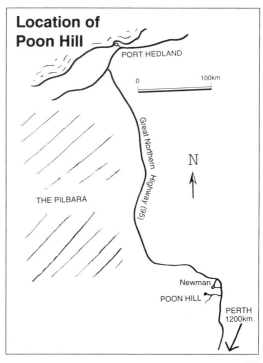

Location of Poon Hill

PORT HEDLAND

0   100km

Great Northern Highway (95)

THE PILBARA

N

Newman

POON HILL

PERTH
1200km

the area. The surprisingly modern town of Newman has a supermarket and petrol station.

Climate and when to go
The only time when the conditions are bearable for climbing at Poon Hill is during the winter (May-Sept). Being situated deep in Western Australia almost directly on the Tropic of Capricorn, other times of the year are very hot and dry.

What to take
A concise rack of small nuts and friends, bolts plates and 1 x 50m rope. Drinking water, a brimmed hat and sunscreen.

Guide to climbs
Contact Mountain Designs.

The best crags of Western Australia have been covered. Although Perth is not renowned as a city of any particular climbing prowess, the following places are a pleasant day's outing from the city.

CHURCHMAN'S BROOK
This has to be the number one choice from Perth. Good length, single pitch climbing comes from this beautifully located granite outcrop.

Geology: Granite

Number of climbs: 60

Grade of climbs: 5-26 (middle grade)

Potential for new routes: Yes (upper grade)

Rock quality: Sound

Protection: Bolts and natural pro

Length of climbs: 5-35m single pitch

Predominant climbing style: All styles

SPORT
Location and Access
From the city follow signs to Armadale on the South Western Highway (20). A few km before Armadale turn left onto the Brookton Highway (40). After 5km turn right onto Soldiers Road, before Roleystone. Continue for 2km until the road flattens, past the Churchman's Brook dam. Turn right onto the dirt track and follow to the end. Park by the fence. A short walk down the track on the right-hand side of the fence leads to the crag.

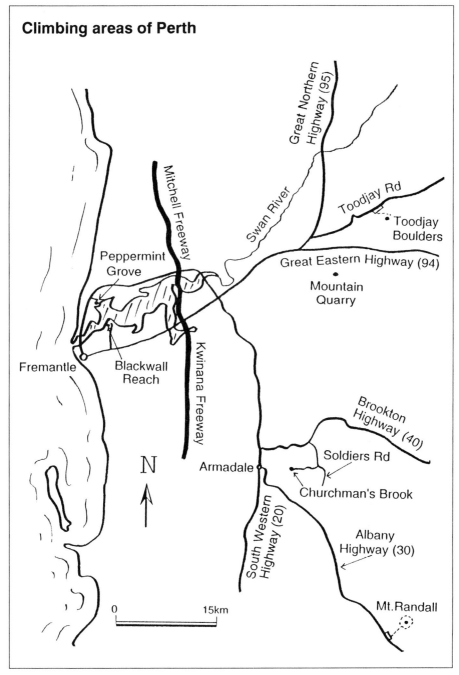

Climbing areas of Perth

Camping and Supplies
There is no camping at Churchman's Brook.

Climate and when to go
Churchman's Brook has all year round climbing, if you can adjust to the seasons. Summer (Nov-Feb) is very hot and dry, taking plenty of water, sunscreen and a hat is a mandatory procedure. The winter months are much cooler and heavy downpours are not uncommon.

Guide to climbs
Contact Mountain Designs.

MOUNT RANDALL

Geology: Granite

Number of climbs: 20

Grade of climbs: 17-23

Potential for new routes: Yes

Rock quality: Sound (very coarse)

Protection: Bolts and natural pro

Length of climbs: 5-20m single pitch

Predominant climbing style: Crack/slab

SPORT

Location and Access (see map p83)
Mount Randall is approximately 60km south of Perth. From the city centre, take the South Western Highway for 28km to Armadale. At Armadale, turn onto the Albany Highway (30). After 31km pull into the roadside just before the Forestry quarantine sign. The summit track to Mount Randall leads from here. 30 minutes of steep walking takes you to the trig point on the top. The climbing is found on the ring of surrounding boulders.

Camping and Supplies
There is no camping at Mount Randall.

Climate and when to go
See Churchman's Brook.

Guide to climbs
Same.

MOUNTAIN QUARRY

Geology: Granite/Dolerite

Number of climbs: 40

Grade of climbs: 5-24

Potential for new routes: No

Rock quality: Fair (beware of loose rock)

Protection: Some bolts, natural pro

Length of climbs: 5-65m single, some multi-pitch

Predominant climbing style: All styles

SPORT

Location and Access (see map p83)

Mountain Quarry is located about 20km outside the city, in the eastern suburb of Boya. Entrance to the quarry is on the left of Coulston Road, not far past the bus stop. Please do not park inside the quarry.

Camping and Supplies

There is no camping at Mountain Quarry.

Climate and when to go

See Churchman's Brook.

Useful information

To climb in Perth quarries a permit must be obtained from the State Planning Commission. Tel 425 7333.

Guide to climbs

Same.

PERTH BOULDERING
BLACKWALL REACH

Probably Perth's best bouldering resort. Steep and overhanging problems are the ticket on this limestone outcrop. There is also an excellent roof where a fall will result as a plunge into the Swan river making a life jacket more suitable than a safety harness!

Location and access (see map p83)

From the city cross the Swan river via the Kwinana Freeway. Turn onto the Canning Highway once on the south bank, heading west towards Fremantle.

85

Continue along the highway for about 10km to the suburb of Bicton, just after Melville. Turn right here into Point Walter Road. Drive north along this through the roundabout for approximately 2km to reach a parking area on the left. Walk 200m north on a concrete footpath, then turn left down a sandy track. Carefully make your way down to the riverside. The roof and bouldering outcrop is obvious on the left.

PEPPERMINT GROVE

Location and Access (see map p83)

Almost directly opposite Blackwall Reach. Peppermint Grove is situated on the north bank of the Swan river 8km to the west of the city centre. Leave the city centre to the west via the Stirling Highway. Drive along for approximately 8km to reach the left turning of McNeil Street into the suburb of Peppermint Grove. Park at the end of McNeil Street, then walk a short distance north up Bindering Parade to find a paved footpath on the right. The climbing face is to be found down this path on the right.

TOODJAY BOULDERS

Location and access (see map p83)

Toodjay Boulders are situated about 25km north-east of Perth. Turn right off the Great Northern Highway onto Toodjay Road. Continue along this for 7.5km, then park in the lay-by near the top of the hill. Walk up the hill on the right (south) side of the road for 5 minutes to reach a cluster of granite boulders. Problems up to 10m are generally slabs and cracks.

Useful addresses

Mountain Designs (gym, equipment)
862 Hay Street
Perth, WA 6000
Tel (09) 322 4774

Western Australia Climbing Gym
Subiaco
Perth WA

Get Vertical (gym)
37 Hector Street
Osborne Park, WA 6017
Tel (09) 242 7230

Paddy Pallin (equipment)
915 Hay Street
Perth, WA
Tel (09) 321 2666

Western Australian
Tourist Centre Corner of Forest Place
& Wellington Street Perth, WA
Tel (09) 482 1111

Department of Conservation & Land
Management, State Operations HQ
50 Hayman Road
Como, WA 6152
Tel (09) 367 0333

Climbing Association WA
PO Box 623 Subiaco WA 6008

WA Tourist Office
92 Pitt Street Sydney 2000
Tel (02) 233 4400

THE NORTHERN TERRITORY

The Northern Territory is a most authentic and intriguing state. It holds some of Australia's most famous landmarks and an unusually diverse climate. There are stunning national parks and forbidden sacred lands to the tropical north, known as the Top End, whereas the southern part of the state, The Red Centre, has many ancient and mystical formations hidden deep in the barren area of this country's almost surreal heart.

Despite what you may assume about this desiccated territory, there are more things to climb than cacti, sand dunes and camels!

NB. The climbing scene in the Northern Territory, as with most of Australia, is still in the development stages. There are many unclimbed areas waiting to be discovered. For cultural and political reasons, Ayers Rock, Kings Canyon and Kakadu National Parks are currently out of bounds to rock climbers. Always contact the local authorities (addresses given) before putting up new routes at any area previously unclimbed.

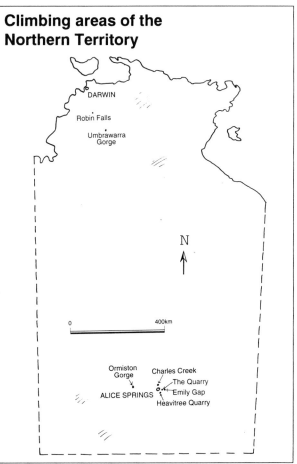

Climbing areas of the Northern Territory

Umbrawarra Gorge, Northern Territory. Photo: Alon Hod

THE TOP END:
UMBRAWARRA GORGE

Umbrawarra Gorge is the Top End's best climbing area. These quality cliffs in a remote and wild location have single pitch climbing high above a series of scenic tropical waterholes which lie at the base of the gorge, justifying a trip this far north.

Geology: Sandstone

Number of climbs: 20

Grade of climbs: 16-22

Potential for new routes: Yes

Rock quality: Good

Protection: Natural gear, few bolts

Length of climbs: 10-25m single pitch

Predominant climbing style: Face, horizontal breaks

Location and Access

240km south of Darwin along the Stuart Highway (1) is the small town of Pine Creek. A further 3km south of Pine Creek is the turn off on the right (west) for the gorge. Umbrawarra Gorge can be found about 12km along this road which is lined with termite hills.

Camping and Supplies
There is a campsite at the entrance to the gorge where facilities include water, toilets and barbecues. Camping fees are cheap. There is also a basic hotel and campsite in the old gold rush town of Pine Creek, where supplies are limited and expensive. Food stocks are best sought in the larger towns of Darwin or Katherine.

Climate and when to go
At the top end the average temperature of 28°C does not fluctuate much throughout the year. The best and only time to visit as far as climbing is concerned

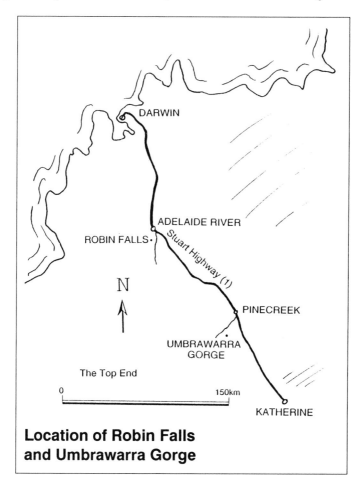

**Location of Robin Falls
and Umbrawarra Gorge**

is during 'the dry season', which generally runs through the winter months Apr-Oct. The rest of the year (Nov-Mar) 'the wet season', as it suggests, has a very high rainfall and frequent thunderstorms.

What to take
A full rack of natural gear, particularly camming devices as bolts are in the minority at this crag. A good water bottle to keep yourself hydrated in the hot humid conditions. A hat, sunscreen and a swimming costume for the waterholes.

Useful information
For more information on climbing at Umbrawarra Gorge contact Snowgum, Bagot Road, Coconut Grove Village, Darwin, NT 0810. Tel (089) 481717.

Author's rating **

Guide to climbs
See above address for latest developments.

ROBIN FALLS

Another little known climbing area at the Top End is at Robin Falls. (see map p89) The falls are located about 15km south of Adelaide River, a town 130km south of Darwin along the Stuart Highway. The climbs are situated about 120m downstream from the falls proper on the right-hand bank. Look for a rock buttress approximately 25m above the stream.

THE RED CENTRE:

This is where the majority of the climbing in the Northern Territory lies, thanks to the parallel ridges of the sun baked Macdonnell Ranges which run practically unbroken for 150 miles and the small but very enthusiastic climbing community of Alice Springs. (Just call out 'Yerba mate' at one of the following crags and you'll see what I mean!)

There is a proliferation of gorges, gaps, bluffs, mounts and ranges, climbed and unclimbed within the area, so don't be afraid of venturing out to discover a secret boulder of your own. The following five climbing areas are the best and most well developed of the Red Centre, offering great climbing in what is a vastly unique landscape.

ORMISTON GORGE

This is Northern Territory's premier cliff which demonstrates the harsh environment of its situation, being in a dry river bed. Apart from the high quality routes there are also beautiful views of the surrounding semi-desert lands.

Geology: Sandstone

Number of climbs: 30

Grade of climbs: 12-22

Potential for new routes: Yes

Rock quality: Good

Protection: Natural gear, bolts

Length of climbs: 6-25m single pitch

Predominant climbing style: All styles

Location and Access

Ormiston Gorge is located 130km west of Alice Springs in the West MacDonnell National Park. Head west from Alice Springs along Larapinta Drive which turns into Namatjira Drive, towards Glen Helen. After 130km, take the turning on the right for Ormiston Gorge. To access one of the best cliffs, Ormiston Bluff, follow the road in towards the gorge until you are past the grid and the river bed is directly on your right. Look for a large steep bluff directly on the other side of the river, 50m walk away. If you pass the Ranger Station you've gone too far. For the climbs in the gorge itself park at the Ranger's Station and walk into the gorge from there.

Camping and Supplies

Camping and water are available by the Ranger's Station at the entrance to the gorge. Be prepared with good stocks of food and fuel from Alice Springs before setting off.

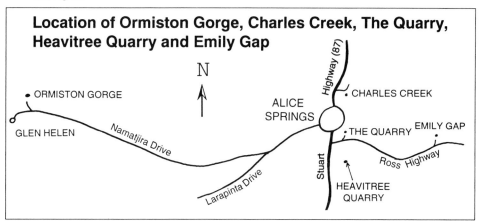

Location of Ormiston Gorge, Charles Creek, The Quarry, Heavitree Quarry and Emily Gap

Climate and when to go

Climbing is possible all year round at Ormiston Gorge, except for the summer months Dec-Feb, where temperatures can soar up to 45°C. Conditions are very dry in the centre, as it has the lowest rainfall in Australia. Also, bring appropriately warm camping gear for the winter as temperatures plummet to only a few degrees at night.

What to take

Full rack of natural gear, sunscreen, a good sized water bottle.

Recommended classics

Old Favourite	18m	20	(Ormiston Bluff)
Step Right Up	20m	21	(Ormiston Bluff)
Sickle	25m	16	(Ormiston Bluff)

Useful information

Please inform the Ranger on duty of your intentions to climb at Ormiston Gorge on (089) 567799. There is some of the best bouldering in the area at the base of the cliff.

Author's rating **

Guide to climbs

Contact Ooraminna Outdoors for latest developments. Tel (08) 89528746.

CHARLES CREEK

If time is limited in Alice Springs, then Charles Creek is the perfect opportunity to squeeze in a few short climbs at this easily accessible cliff.

Geology: Quartzite

Number of climbs: 15

Grade of climbs: 11-21

Potential for new routes: Yes

Rock quality: Sound

Protection: Bolts, some natural gear

Length of climbs: 6-10m

Predominant climbing style: Face, crack

SPORT

Location and Access (see map p91)

Charles Creek is located within the Telegraph Station Conservation Reserve 5km north of Alice Springs. From the northbound Stuart Highway (87) out of Alice Springs, turn right onto a dirt track directly after the 'Welcome to Thank you for visiting Alice Springs' sign (just before the Charles River Bridge). Follow the dirt track (Old North Road) to the top of the rise and park where the track takes a sharp left and heads downhill under the bridge. The cliff is down on your right east in the dry creek bed about 50m below.

Camping and Supplies

Camping is not available at Charles Creek. There are a good selection of hostels, guesthouses, supermarkets, campsites and caravan parks in and around Alice Springs.

Climate and when to go

The best time to visit Charles Creek is during the more agreeable conditions during Feb-Dec.

Recommended classics

Face Value	10m	20
Smear Madness	10m	18

What to take

Quickdraws, bolt plates, the odd friend placement. Most routes have bolt runners or fixed hangers with double bolt belays. Plenty of water as none is available at the crag. A hat, sunscreen. A canoe in case of flash floods!

Useful information

For more information on climbing at Charles Creek contact Ooraminna Outdoors. Tel (08) 89528746.

Guide to climbs

Try buying a copy of the local climbing magazine *Crankit* for the latest route descriptions and developments.

HEAVITREE QUARRY

Geology: Sandstone

Number of climbs: 12

Grade of climbs: 15-24

Potential for new routes: Yes

Rock quality: Sound

Protection: Natural gear, bolts

Length of climbs: 10-15m

Predominant climbing style: Face, crack

SPORT

Location and Access (see map p91)

Exit Alice Springs on the south Stuart Highway (87) and drive through Heavitree Gap. Take the first turn left and drive past several caravan parks to a roundabout. Turn left here on to Rapinesi Road. Follow this to the end where you turn left again. Drive past the horse stables to the gates of the quarry. Park on the left. Don't drive into the quarry as the gates may be locked with you inside. Walk uphill to the right for approximately 400m to the obvious orange wall featuring some inviting cracks.

Camping and Supplies

Camping is not allowed at Heavitree Quarry.

Climate and when to go

Climbing is possible all year round at Heavitree Quarry, however be cautious of hot days during the summer months (Dec-Feb) when it can get extremely hot as early as 10am.

Recommended classics

Superstring	15m	24
First Temptation	15m	24

What to take

A rack of natural gear, bolt plates. Plenty of water. A hat and sunscreen.

Useful information

There is also some good bouldering on the rocks up the hill towards the cliff.

Guide to climbs

As before.

THE QUARRY

SPORT

This is the Red Centre's sport climbing capital. Basically a steep red wall offering hard sustained climbing of grades 19-24. From Alice Springs head east on the Ross Highway. After approximately 1km turn left into Quarry Road (signposted Aussie's

Trail Rides). Continue to the gates of the quarry and park at the side of the road. The cliff is a 15 minute walk up the scree to the right. The quarry is a lovely place to be, particularly at sunset, as it has attractive views overlooking Alice Springs.

EMILY GAP

This scenic spot is popular with climbers and picnickers alike. Capturing some of Australia's heritage with cave paintings and beautiful fig trees, Emily Gap provides some of the centre's best easy single and multi-pitch traditional climbing.

Geology: Sandstone

Number of climbs: 30

Grade of climbs: 11-17

Potential for new routes: Yes

Rock quality: Fair

Protection: Natural gear

Length of climbs: 12-65m

Predominant climbing style: Face, crack, slab, corner

Location and Access (see map p91)
Emily Gap is located 16km to the east of Alice Springs, just off the Ross Highway (signposted). The main cliff is only a short walk from the car park.

Camping and Supplies
There is no camping allowed at Emily Gap.

Climate and when to go
See other climbing areas of the Red Centre.

Recommended classics
Amaronthine	52m	12
Handle with Care	65m	15

What to take
1 x 50m rope as the 2 pitch climbs do not require abseils but have descent tracks. A full rack of natural gear. Water as none is available. A hat and sunscreen.

Useful information
Please respect and treat the land and cliffs of Emily Gap considerately as this is a sacred area to the Aborigines. Bolting is definitely out.

Guide to climbs
As before.

Other climbing areas in the Red Centre to look out for include: Glen Helen Gorge, Serpentine Gorge, The Unknown Trephina Gorge, Jesse Gap and the very isolated yet impressive mesa of Mount Connor.

Useful addresses

Central Australia YMCA (gym)
Sadadeen Road
Alice springs
NT 0870
Tel (08) 52 5666

Ooraminna Outdoors (equipment)
Alice Springs
NT
Tel (08) 895 28746

Snowgum (equipment)
Bagot Road
Coconut Grove Village
Darwin
NT 0810
Tel (089) 481717

Conservation Commission of
Northern Territory
Arid Zone Research Institute
South Stuart Highway
Alice Springs, NT 8070
Tel (089) 51 8211

National Parks & Wildlife Service
Darwin
NT
Tel (089) 815299

The Northern Territory Government
Tourist Bureau
31 Smith Street
Darwin
NT
Tel (089) 816611

and

Plaza Building
Todd St Mall
Alice Springs
NT
Tel (089) 52 1299

Klaus Klein climbing the granite sea cliffs of Willyabrup (Margaret River), Western Australia

Sandstone escarpments of the Blue Mountains, New South Wales *Photo Klaus Klein*
Andrew Bull on Silent Rage (25), Boronia Point, Blue Mountains *Photo Klaus Klein*

QUEENSLAND

The reasons for travelling to Queensland's east coast may not only be to visit some of Australia's hottest rock. A surfers' paradise, with diving on the Great Barrier Reef, and tropical rainforests of the far north, this holiday state has a lot to offer. Travelling is easy through these fertile and relatively populated lands. The two great Queensland crags have a typical Australian grandeur. Kings could not have positioned castles more strategically, such is their dominance over the surrounding settlements. Winter is the time to visit Queensland as the wet season is Dec-Apr.

MOUNT STUART

Mount Stuart is north Queensland's best and most developed cliff. This quality escarpment stands high on steep bushlands, 500m clear of the skirting coastal lands. Routes are superbly exposed by aerial views over the city of Townsville, blissfully surrounded by the glistening coral sea. The extensive cliffline at Mount Stuart is unique. It has the easily accessible short bolted climbs of an all comers sport crag (The Playground) alongside the longer buttress and turrets found further afield that will satisfy any pioneering spirit (The Mainfaces/Colorado Wall).

Geology: Granite/Sandstone mix

Number of climbs: 150

Grade of climbs: 10-26 (middle grade)

Potential for new routes: Yes, multi-pitch

Rock quality: Good

Protection: Bolts and natural pro

Length of climbs: 10-100m mostly single pitch, some multi

Predominant climbing style: Face, corner, arête

SPORT

Location and Access

Mount Stuart is the obvious mountain with TV antennae on top to the south of Townsville on the north-east coast of Queensland. Exit the city to the south via Charter Towers - Bowen Road. This turns into the Flinders Highway (78). Take the right turn after approximately 15km to the Mount Stuart summit (signposted). Follow the narrow winding road for approximately 10km almost until the top. At the fork in the road, do not turn left to the picnic area and summit, instead continue right to the TV antennae fencing. Park on the left without blocking the gate. A 5 minute walk along the track that follows the mesh fencing will bring you to a rock plateau. This is the top of the main climbing area The Playground. There are descent gullies at both ends of the cliff to access the base of the crags. To reach

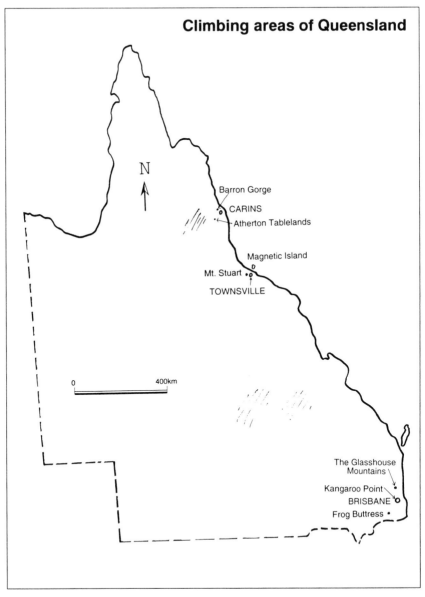

Climbing areas of Queensland

N

Barron Gorge

CARINS

Atherton Tablelands

Magnetic Island

Mt. Stuart

TOWNSVILLE

0   400km

The Glasshouse Mountains

Kangaroo Point

BRISBANE

Frog Buttress

the longer multi-pitch climbs of The Main Faces and Colorado Wall, a longer, more adventurous approach is required along the base of the cliffs to the north of the outcrop.

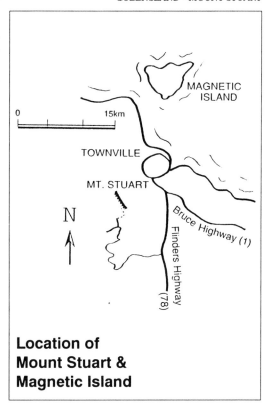

Camping and Supplies

Camping is allowed on the rock plateau above The Playground, but there are no facilities on Mount Stuart. Take plenty of drinking water, deal with human refuse in the correct manner and take all your rubbish with you. Alternatively there is a choice of three camp/caravan parks, all close to Townsville. Townsville has a large supermarket and several petrol stations.

Location of Mount Stuart & Magnetic Island

Climate and when to go

Climbing at Mount Stuart is best between the drier, cooler winter months of May and Oct (temperature mid to high 20s!). Other times of year are too hot and wet.

What to take

A good selection of wires and friends, long slings and locking carabiners for wrapping round boulders to make anchors. Bolt plates. Lots of drinking water. A good hat and sunscreen.

Recommended classics

Yankee Logic	22m	21	(The Playground)
Cannon Ball	22m	17	(The Playground)
Eye of the Tiger	20m	17	(The Playground)
A Separate Reality	20m	23	(The Playground)
Romancing the Stone	50m	22	(The Pinnacle)
Cosmic Messenger	80m	23	(The Main Faces)
A Few Good Men	80m	24	(Colorado Wall)

Mount Stuart, Queensland. Photo: Max Bretherton

Useful information

Townsville Information Centre, Flinders Street Mall, Townsville, QLD.
Tel (077) 712 724.

For more information contact Adventure Equipment, 11 Ross River Road,
Townsville, QLD. Tel (077) 756 116.

Greetings from Max Bretherton on the pinnacle, Mount Stuart. Photo: Alastair Lee

Author's rating **

Guide to climbs

Mount Stuart Climbing Guide by the Professional Association of Climbing Instructors (1995)

101

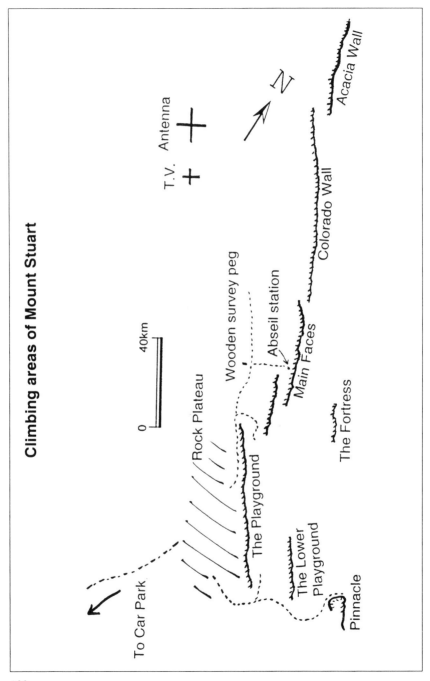

Climbing areas of Mount Stuart

MAGNETIC ISLAND

Magnetic Island is a beautiful reef island popular with travellers, just 13km offshore from Townsville. There are numerous bays along the island's coast where hundreds of perfect granite boulders are to be found guarding the ends of each cove. Outcrops and buttresses are also frequent sightings on the bushland hills and coastal walks, tantamount to a climber's paradise.

At present there have been very few climbing trips to Magnetic Island, with only a handful of top roped first ascents on The Lizard (an impressive 25m buttress on the sea front, 1 hour's walk west from Horseshoe Bay). Other groups have spent many a happy day exploring and bouldering one of the many bays. Undeveloped and undocumented, the potential of this bouldering wonderland is there for whoever claims it.

There is a regular bus service that connects with the ferry between the north and south of the 7km long island. Good bushwalking tracks make easy access over the hills and along the coast to reach the bays. The north-east of the island is particularly good. Look out for Horseshoe, Bolding and Radical Bays and Rocky Bay to the south. Happy exploring!

Useful information

Camping and supplies are available on the island. As for Mount Stuart, winter has very pleasant conditions. Also take a landing pad.

BARRON GORGE

This little known climbing area has been included in this guide simply to warn the unsuspecting not to go. The number of established routes hardly breaks into double figures. The routes on The Monument in particular are short and gnarly. It is not worth the journey this far north, solely to climb at Barron Gorge. Only with a tour to the likes of Cape Tribulation or the Great Barrier Reef from Cairns, extending to the far north of Queensland as part of the itinerary, and with a desperate urge to climb, would the Barron Gorge be an option! Having said that, it is a pretty area, with lots of waterfalls and thick green rainforests.

Geology: Strange conglomerate (granite/limestone?)

Number of climbs: 12

Grade of climbs: 16-22

Potential for new routes: Yes, at the falls

Rock quality: Sound

Protection: Bolts and natural pro

Length of climbs: 5-25m

103

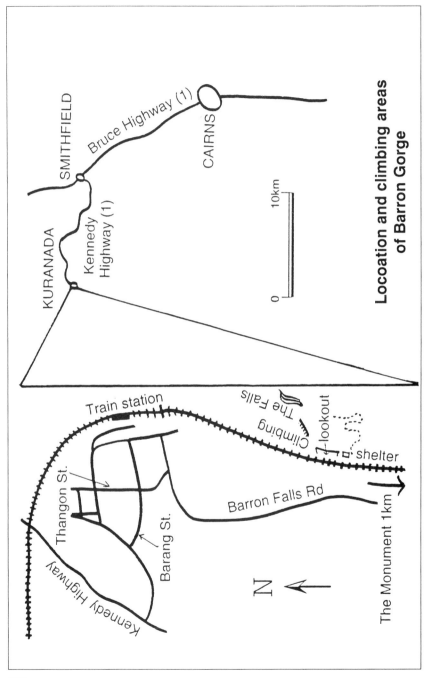

Locoation and climbing areas of Barron Gorge

Predominant climbing style: Face, crack corner

SPORT

Location and Access
The Barron Gorge National Park is located 20km west of Cairns near the town of Kuranda. Head north from Cairns on Highway 1. After 13km turn left at Smithfield onto the Kennedy Highway. Approximately 10km of steep road leads to the left turning for Kuranda town centre. From this road leading to the town, turn right onto Barang Street, then right onto Thangon Street and then right onto Barron Falls Road. A short distance along Barron Falls Road turn left to the falls lookout. Park here. There are a few natural pro routes at the base of the gorge itself. To access them, cross over the railway line (watch for trains!) and find a disused track behind the shelter on the right of the lookout platform. This is a very steep and precarious track; take great care in descending it. Ten minutes will bring you to the end of the track near the base of the falls. There is a face with a central buttress to the left and in front (standing facing the falls). Some fixed protection (carabiners and slings are visible from this point at the top of the buttress).

To access the bolted climbs on a short monolith called The Monument, walk 1km down the track south (again look out for trains). The Monument is on the left at the top of the embankment. There are belay chains on the top.

Camping and Supplies
There is no camping in Barron Gorge National Park.

Climate and when to go
The warm and drier weather away from the 'wet season' between May and Oct is the best time to visit the Barron Gorge. The rest of the year is hot and very wet.

What to take
Set of wires and friends, bolt plates, 1 x 50m rope. Drinking water.

Useful information
For more information on climbing at Barron Gorge contact Adventure Equipment, 69 Grafton Street, Cairns, QLD 4870. Tel (070) 312 669 Fax 31 1384.

Author's rating Don't go!

Guide to climbs
There is no guide currently available.

THE ATHERTON TABLELANDS

A much better option for climbing in North Queensland is this beautiful uprising which stretches between Cairns and Innisfail. Little is known about climbing in the tablelands other than it is there. Many first ascents of long natural lines have been taken but there is still a huge potential on the high escarpments of this lush rainforest plateau. For latest developments contact Adventure Equipment, 69 Grafton Street, Cairns, QLD 4870. Tel (070) 312 669 Fax 31 1384.

GLASSHOUSE MOUNTAINS

Quite an amazing spectacle, basically a line of volcanic mounds and spires protruding clear of the southern Queensland farmlands. The crags are popular with aid and free climbers alike. The Glasshouse Mountains have good variety in length, style and difficulty of routes, the majority being easy grade multi-pitch adventure climbing. Nevertheless do not be misled by the word 'easy'. Climbs in the Glasshouse Mountains are very serious undertakings. Routes can be very long (up to 350m) and time-consuming affairs. Experience in gear placement and routefinding are essential skills for the often loose, run out and exposed climbing on these cliffs.

The four main areas of the GHM are as follows.

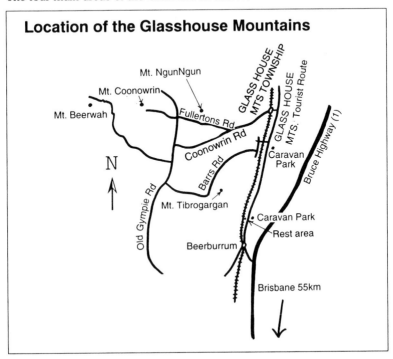

Location of the Glasshouse Mountains

MOUNT BEERWAH

Geology: Volcanic

Number of climbs: 20

Grade of climbs: 1-16

Potential for new routes: Yes

Rock quality: Fair

Protection: Bolts (on aid routes), natural pro

Length of climbs: 30-350m multi-pitch

Predominant climbing style: Aid (all styles)

Location and Access (see map p106)

The Glasshouse Mountains National Park is 65km north of Brisbane. Head north from Brisbane for 55km along the Bruce Highway, then turn left onto the signposted Glasshouse Mountains tourist route. Proceed along this road for 10km passing through the village of Beerburrum to reach Glasshouse town by turning left. Mount Beerwah is a short drive from here. After crossing the railway line turn left onto Coonowrin Road. Continue to the end and turn left onto Old Gympie Road. The next right leads onto a dirt road that ends at the Mount Beerwah National Park picnic area and car park (signposted) (refer to map). From the car park climbs are between 15 minutes' and 1 hour's walks on good tracks (some steep scrambles) to the north, east and west faces.

Camping and Supplies

Camping is not allowed within any of the Glasshouse Mountains National Parks. There are camping/caravan parks along the Glasshouse Mountain tourist route between Beerburrum and Glasshouse town. There is also a free overnight rest area with toilets and water, just off the tourist route near Beerburrum. Food and fuel is available at the small township along the tourist route. Of course a cheaper option is to stock up in the large supermarkets in Brisbane or Gympie if arriving from the north.

Climate and when to go

Year round climbing is possible at the Glasshouse Mountains. Winter (May-Sept) is temperate, rarely dropping below 15°C, whereas summer (Nov-Feb) can break into the 30°Cs, making climbing, specifically in the sun, very hot. Heavy storms are also quite frequent during summer.

What to take

As much gear as you can lay your hands on. Two x 50m ropes work well on the long climbs at Mount Beerwah. A helmet is also well advised. Plenty of water and sunscreen (toilets and water available at Mount Beerwah NP).

Useful information
Many of the routes in the Glasshouse Mountains were set in the 1960s, therefore the old and corroding piton runners found at some belay points are not to be trusted.

Guide to climbs
A Guidebook to Rock Climbing on the Glasshouse Mountains by Col Smithies (1994)

MOUNT COONOWRIN (CROOKNECK)
Geology: Volcanic

Number of climbs: 40

Grade of climbs: 3-24 (hard/middle)

Potential for new routes: No

Rock quality: Sound

Protection: Bolts and natural pro

Length of climbs: 10-100m single, some multi-pitch

Predominant climbing style: Face, roof, arête, crack, corner

Location and Access (see map p106)
From the Glasshouse Mountains tourist route, turn left to Glasshouse town. Go across the railway track, turn left onto Coonowrin Road, follow this to the end, then turn right onto Old Gympie Road. After about 1km turn left into Fullertons Road. 1km of this road takes you to the National Park car park (approximately a 10 minute journey) (Refer to map). A short walk along the track leading from the car park leads to the base of the cliffs. The popular areas of the south (left) and east (right) faces are accessible from this point. 'Easier' multi-pitch climbs can be found on the north and west faces.

What to take
For the single-pitch climbs, wires, friends and bolt plates, slings. 1 x 50m rope. Plenty of water (not available at this park) (no toilets).

MOUNT NGUN NGUN

Geology: Volcanic
Number of climbs: 100
Grade of climbs: 10-24
Potential for new routes: Yes
Rock quality: Sound
Protection: Bolts and natural pro
Length of climbs: 10-50m single-pitch
Predominant climbing style: All styles
SPORT

Location and Access (see map p106)
From the Glasshouse Mountain tourist route turn left to Glasshouse town. Go across the railway track and turn left onto Coonowrin Road. After 1km turn right into Fullertons Road. The National Park car park is about 1.5km on the right of this road (5 minutes journey) (refer to map) A good walking track leads from the car park. Follow this, passing a cave up to the plateau. Follow the main track for a further 100m, then a small white arrow shows a left branching track. This will take you to the main climbing area (the upper south/face) of Mount Ngun ngun.

Author's rating *

What to take
For a single-pitch climb, wires, friends and bolt plates, slings, 1 x 50m rope. Take water, available at car park.

MOUNT TIBROGARGAN

Geology: Volcanic
Number of climbs: 40
Grade of climbs: 4-24 (easy)
Potential for new routes: Yes
Rock quality: Fair
Protection: Natural pro
Length of climbs: 20-350m, mostly multi-pitch
Predominant climbing style: Crack, face, slab, corner, chimney, roof

Location and Access (see map p106)
Drive north for 5km along the Glasshouse Mountain tourist route from Beerburrum. Turn left over the railway track and left again onto Railway Parade, then turn right into Barrs Road. This will take you to the National Park picnic area on the west side of Mount Tibrogargan, a 10 minute journey. Tracks to the north-west, north, north-east, east, south-east, south and west faces all lead from here around the mountain (refer to map).

What to take
Full rack of wires, friends, slings, 2 x 50m ropes for the often wandering multi-pitches. Drinking water (there are toilets, but no water).

For more information on the Glasshouse Mountains contact the ranger:

QNPWS	QNPWS
Beerwah Office	North Coast Area Office
Roys Road	PO Box 697
Beerwah, QLD 4519	Gympie, QLD 4570
Tel (074) 94 6630	Tel (074) 82 4189

FROG BUTTRESS

This superb location is the 'promised land' of Australian crack climbing. Quality climbs are in abundance on this compact columnar scarp of the Mount French NP. Looking beautifully across the rural base of the Fassifern Valley, the cliffs have unrivalled access combined with easy route location. Frog Buttress is undeniably one of Australia's best crags.

> **Geology:** Rhyolite
>
> **Number of climbs:** 300
>
> **Grade of climbs:** 5-32
>
> **Potential for new routes:** No
>
> **Rock quality:** Good
>
> **Protection:** Bolts, mostly natural pro
>
> **Length of climbs:** 5-50m, 1 and 2 pitch
>
> **Predominant climbing style:** Crack

Location and Access
Frog Buttress is located 100km south and west of Brisbane in the Mount French National Park. The quickest way is west on Highway 2 from the city. 30km bring you to a left turn onto the southern Ipswich bypass, which joins to the south heading Cunningham Highway (15). Continue along this for 40km, taking a

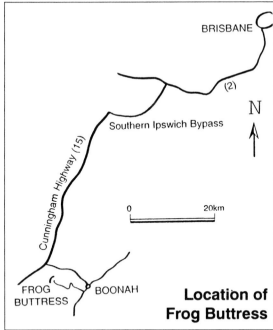

Location of Frog Buttress

signposted left turn to Boonah. Once in Boonah stay on the main road, driving through the town past the shopping centre, heading south for 1km. The right turn for Mount French National Park is signposted next to the Dugandan Hotel. Follow the signs and steep road to reach the camping and car park on the forested summit.

The climbing can be found a short walk away, along the path to the scree slope (descent track) which is between the two cliffs.

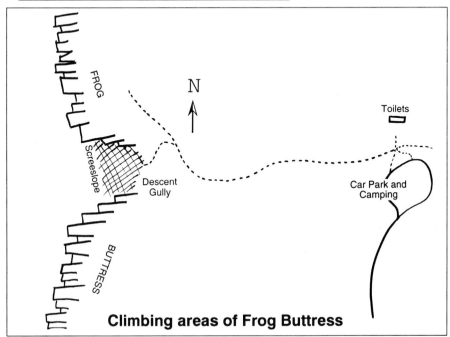

Climbing areas of Frog Buttress

Camping and Supplies

Camping is allowed at Frog Buttress. Amenities include toilets, tap water, fire places and picnic tables. Fees are payable. The local town of Boonah has a supermarket, bank, petrol station, laundry and climbing shop.

Climate and when to go

Climbing is possible between Feb and Nov at Frog Buttress, with the most comfortable times being spring (Sept-Nov) and autumn (Feb-May). Summer is very hot and often wet, whereas winter can be a little cool. The nights in particular are cold.

What to take

A healthy crack climbing rack, wires, friends, hexes, slings, 2 x 50m ropes. Bolt plates for harder routes. Tape for hand jamming. Although the rock at Frog Buttress rarely breaks, there are a lot of loose boulders, rock and stones on the steep slopes at the top of the cliffs. Helmets are advised. A ground sheet to protect the rope from the dusty surface of the ground.

Recommended classics

Whistling Kite	32	30m
Blood, Sweat and Tears	15	40m
Piranha	20	45m
Clockwork Orange	13	15m
Nemesis	19	25m
Impulse	24	18m
Satan's Smokestack	16	40m

Useful information

Most climbs at Frog Buttress are easily located by the initial of each climb marked at the base of the cliffs.

For more information contact: 'The crags', High Street, Boonah, QLD.
Tel (074) 63 2863 Fax (074) 63 2958

Author's rating***

Guide to climbs

A Guidebook to Rockclimbing Frog Buttress by Col Smithies (1995)

KANGAROO POINT

This old urban quarry is the definitive city crag. Situated on the banks of the

Brisbane river, the cliffs look across to the office blocks and skyscrapers of a central business district. The attractions of Kangaroo Point include lots of great climbs, concrete bollard anchors along the top of the cliff line, free electric barbecues, and parking a few yards from the belay railing. To round off this user friendly outdoor gym, the rock is also floodlit until the early hours of each morning.

Geology: Sandstone

Number of climbs: 200

Grade of climbs: 3-26

Potential for new routes: No

Rock quality: Sound

Protection: Bolts, natural pro

Length of climbs: 10-20m single-pitch

Predominant climbing style: Face

SPORT

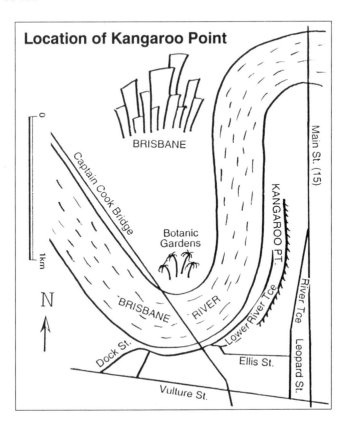

Location of Kangaroo Point

Location and Access (see map p113)
Kangaroo Point is in the heart of the city of Brisbane, by the river, to the east of the Captain Cook bridge. If heading south on Main Street (15) in the suburb of Kangaroo Point, veer right onto the River Terrace. This turns into Leopard Street. Take the second right, Ellis Street, which leads to Lower River Terrace. The cliffs are a few metres from the parking here.

Camping and Supplies
Tent camping is illegal within a 22km radius of Brisbane city centre, therefore camping at Kangaroo Point is not permitted. Travellers making overnight stops in their campervans on the River Terrace car park is not unheard of; however this guide does not advise or encourage this. Facilities include toilets, drinking water and free barbecues.

Alternatively there is a hostel in the suburb of Kangaroo Point, Backpackers Brisbane Central, at 200 Main Street, KP. Tel (07) 891 1434.

Climate and when to go
Year round climbing is possible at Kangaroo Point, with the most temperate weather in winter and spring (May-Nov). In summer the cliffs are in direct sunlight making for unclimbable conditions, taking advantage of the floodlights which are on until past midnight is required at this time of year. Weekends are very busy and parking can be hard to come by, this may or may not be a good time to go depending on whether you like crowds.

What to take
Kangaroo Point is a top roping haven. In that respect only slings, locking carabiners and a rope are required. (Longer slings are better as the anchors can be a few metres from the cliff edge.) For sport leading take bolt plates. There are also plenty of natural leads, where the usual nuts and friends do the job.

Recommended classics

Fowl Deeds in the Chookhouse	20m	23
The Olos Slab	20m	25
Halva	18m	16
The Stoats Stepped Out	18m	21
Brisbane Bitter	18m	24
Cucumber Castle	18m	23

Useful information
For more information on climbing at Kangaroo Point contact Mountain Designs, 105 Albert Street, Brisbane 4000, or the Greater Brisbane Tourist Association, level 2, The Transit Centre, Brisbane. Tel (07) 236 2020.

Guide to climbs
Kangaroo Point Climbing Guide by Neil Monteith (1995)

Useful addresses

Rocksports (climbing gym)
The Factory
224 Barry Pde
Fortitude Valley
Brisbane, QLD 4006
Tel (07) 216 0482

Rocknazium (gym)
Sunnybank Hills Fitness Centre
Shop5, Level 4, Sunnybank Hills,
Shopping Town corner Compton
and Callamods
Sunnybank Hills, QLD 4109
Tel (07) 272 0148

Queensland Climbing Centres
PO Box 930
Palm Beach
QLD 4221
Tel (07) 5593 6919

Mountain Designs (equipment)
105 Albert Street
Brisbane 4000
Tel (07) 221 6756

224 Barry Pde
Fortitude Valley
Tel (07) 216 0462

Adventure Equipment
11 Ross River Road
Townsville, QLD
Tel (077) 756 116

K2 Base Camp (equipment)
140 Wickham Street
Fortitude Valley
Tel (07) 854 1340

The Crags (equipment)
15 High Street
Boonah 4310
Tel (07) 632 863

Adventure Equipment
69 Grafton Street
Cairns, QLD 4870
Tel (07) 31 2669

Queensland National Parks and Wildlife
Service
160 Ann Street
Brisbane, QLD 400
Tel (07) 227 8185

The Queensland Government Travel
Centre
corner of Adelaide and Edward Streets
Brisbane, QLD
Tel (07) 221 6111

Queensland Tourist and Travel
Corporation
75 Castlereagh Street
Sydney, NSW 2000
Tel (02) 232 1788

NEW SOUTH WALES

A lifetime's climbing exists in New South Wales. The huge array of sandstone climbing (in particular) is as varied and diverse as the land it is on. Sydney is the suburban climbing capital. There are sea cliffs of a world standard, the country's highest concentration of hard climbs, sport crags abound on the deep valleys of the Blue Mountains, and for the more traditionally minded, the Warrumbungles or Bungonia Gorge house some of Australia's longest adventure climbs. Climbing is popular and well developed in New South Wales, where Sydney will serve as an excellent centre for sampling Australian climbing.

The Blue Mountains
The Blue Mountains is a fantastic national park, high on the Great Dividing range. The multitude of vast and deep valleys offer spectacular views from the overlooking escarpments of quality sandstone. Short sport climbs are one of the Blueys' fortés.

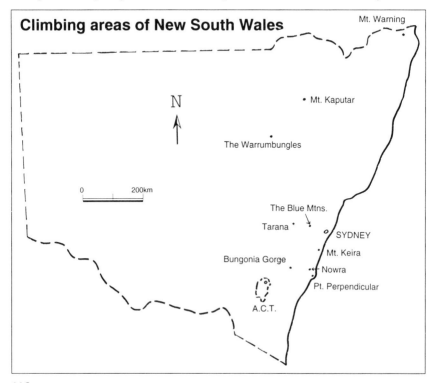

Climbing areas of New South Wales

Many a classic is to be found where hundreds of metres of exposure is experienced on 20m and 30m routes. However, all styles and lengths of climbing can be found under the misty azure radiated by the eucalyptus trees, which flourish throughout the park.

The number of developed climbing areas currently stands at around 35, with every local enthusiast having a 'secret crag' of his own. To list all of these goes beyond the scope of this guidebook. The following areas have been carefully selected and are deemed to be the best crags in the Blue Mountains.

NB. Directions for all Blue Mountains crags are given from the tourist town of Katoomba, which is approximately 100km west of Sydney. From the city head west on Highway 5 to join the Western Motorway which in turn joins the Great Western Highway, which leads to Katoomba. It is a well signposted route which takes about $1^{1/4}$hours.

The Blue Mountains by train

As for most crags in Australia your own transport or an arranged lift is the best and sometimes only way to reach a destination. Fortunately the mainline train west from Sydney goes through the mountains, where there are a couple of stops not too far from the crags. Trains run hourly during the week (Mon-Fri). A good service, although not quite so regular, is available at the weekend. The train from Sydney to Katoomba takes approximately 2 hours.

The three stations of importance in the mountains are Katoomba (15 minute walk to the Three Sisters), Blackheath (20 minute walk to Blackheath area) and Mount Victoria (Mount Piddington, 30 minute walk and Mount York, $1^{1/2}$ hours walk). By following the maps and directions under the location and access sections the crags are easily located on foot. For Mount York from Mount Victoria station, hitching will help reduce the time it takes to cover the 6km journey.

Climate and when to go

The most idyllic times to take a trip to the Blue Mountains are spring (Sept-Nov) and autumn (Feb-May). Climbing is possible during the very hot summer, especially in the morning when most crags lie in the shade. Always take plenty of water, a brimmed hat and sunscreen when climbing, more so in the summer. Climbing in winter is possible on the occasional mild day and sunny afternoon, but on the whole is not recommended. The mountains have an elevation of up to 1000m where winter temperatures can sink to freezing.

Useful information

For more information on climbing in the Blue Mountains contact Mountain Designs, 190 Katoomba Street, Katoomba. Tel (047) 82 5999 or 499 Kent Street, Sydney. Tel (02) 267 3822.

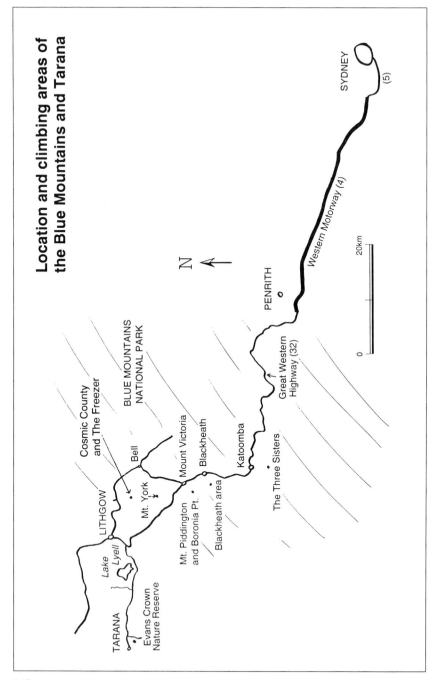

Guide to climbs

The Blue Mountains, a Guide to Selected Rock Climbs by Michael Law (1994). There are three separate guides to Mount Piddington, Cosmic County and the Wolgan Valley by Andrew Penney.

THE THREE SISTERS

The Three Sisters are the Blue Mountains' and one of Australia's top tourist attractions. These adjoining pillars of yellow sandstone offer gripping exposure in a spectacular setting. There are two popular classics worthy of ascension, The Mantleshelf, 20m (13) and West Wall, 160m (12). The second of the two is an easy adventure style of multi-pitch, a rare find in the Blueys.

Geology: Sandstone

Number of climbs: 2

Grade of climbs: 12,13

Potential for new routes: No

Rock quality: Sound

Protection: Bolt belays, natural pro

Length of climbs: 20m, 160m single and multi-pitch

Predominant climbing style: Chimney, crack, slab, face

Location and Access

Drive south down the main street in Katoomba to pick up signs for a short drive to the Three Sisters car park and lookout, called Echo Point. To access the climbs from here walk behind the tourist information to find the top of the giant staircase. Walk down this to find the bridge connecting the first sister. The start of the superb Mantleshelf starts just over the bridge and finishes on the summit of the first sister where a log book can be filled in.

To reach West Wall (about 15 minutes' walking) go to the bottom of the giant staircase to meet the Federal Pass track. Turn right here and follow the track around the nose to the opposite side of the sisters. Look out for a tree on the left, marked WW. Turn right here up a rough track to the base of the cliff. Continue left along the cliff line to reach a metal sign warning against climbing on the east face. The chimney behind this sign is the start of West Wall.

Camping and Supplies

Camping is available not far from the Three Sisters to the west of the main street at Katoomba Falls caravan park, Tel (047) 82 1835, on Katoomba Falls road. A good selection of hostels, lodges and hotels can also be found in Katoomba. The town is well supplied with stores, cafés and petrol stations, satisfying your everyday needs.

What to take

A good rack of nuts and friends, quickdraws (10) and slings. Bolt plates are required for the belay stations. Two x 50m ropes make the abseils more comfortable.

Author's rating **

Recommended classics

The Mantleshelf	20m	(13)
West Wall	160m	(12)

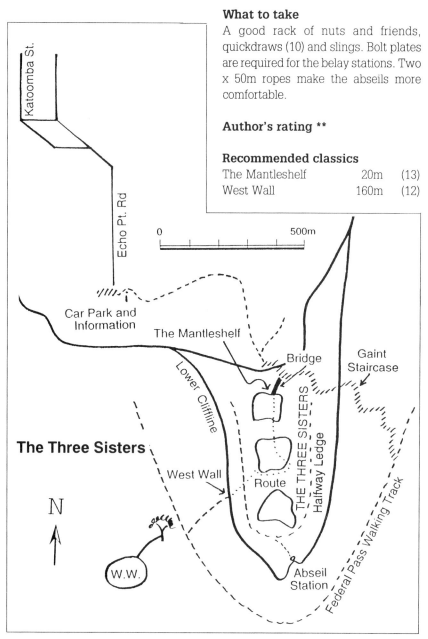

BLACKHEATH

The following crags are in the Blackheath area and all lie within close proximity to each other. These are some of the mountain's most popular sport climbing areas, boasting classic Blue Mountain scenery, excellent rock and easy access. If you are travelling alone this is a good place to meet other climbers to team up with.

Geology: Sandstone

Number of climbs: 200

Grade of climbs: 16-29 (middle, hard)

Potential for new routes: No

Rock quality: Excellent

Protection: Mainly bolts, some natural pro

Length of climbs: 10-70m single pitch, few 2 pitch

SPORT

Location and Access (see map p122)

The small town of Blackheath is 12km further north along the Great Western Highway. At the crossroads in the town centre, turn left into the level crossing. Once over the track take the immediate left. After a few hundred metres turn right into Shipley Road. Follow this for 1km to turn right into the gravel road of Centennial Glen. Park at the end.

Camping and Supplies

Camping is possible in the Blackheath Glen Reserve 5km down the Megalong Valley Road on the right-hand side at the bottom of the hill (a car is needed) or there is the Blackheath caravan park on Prince Edward Street, Tel (047) 87 8101. Supplies are obtainable from Blackheath's take-aways, bakery, general store, off licence and petrol station.

SHIPLEY LOWER

What to take

2 x 50m ropes 10 bolt brackets, a rack of wires, SLCD and friends are very useful here.

Recommended classics

Clockwork Orange	61m	(20)
Nuclear Winter	45m	(24)

Potential for new routes: Yes, high grades.

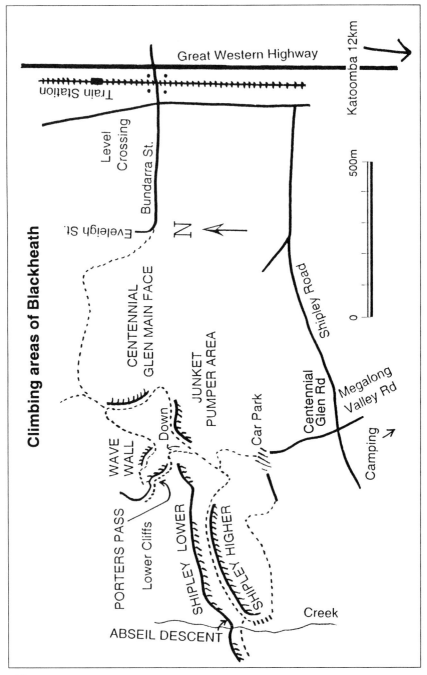

Climbing areas of Blackheath

Alon Hod on Flaming Flamingos (24), Shipley Upper,
Blue Mountains. Photo: Dave Allan

SHIPLEY UPPER

A great face climbing cliff just 5 minutes' walk from the car park (see map). Delicate
moves, excellent rock. Plenty of bolts and lovely exposure all contribute to making
Shipley Upper a popular Blue Mountains choice.

123

What to take

1 x 50m rope, 8-10 bolt plates, small SLCDs required for some routes.

Author's rating *

Recommended classics

Flaming Flamingo	35m	(24)
Country Special	18m	(20S)

PORTERS PASS

This is stepping into the real hard (strong) man's territory. The climbs are long single pitches on typical features and overhangs. Porters Pass is 10 minutes' walk from the car park (see map p122).

What to take

2 x 50m ropes for 30m+ abseils, 10 bolt plates, SLCD and friends required for some routes.

Recommended Classics

Black Heathen	42m	26
SSCC 4	50m	24

CENTENNIAL GLEN: JUNKET PUMPER AREA, MAIN FACE AND WAVE WALL

If you like sport climbing, you've come to the right place. Lots of short, steep, well bolted climbing usually in the upper grades. A very popular area, almost overrun at times, offering thrutchy and powerful moves on good overhanging solid sandstone in sheltered conditions. The Wave Wall in particular has good exposure, with views over the valley across to the Shipley cliffs. Walking time to the cliffs from the car park varies between 10 and 20 minutes (see map) p122.

What to take

1 x 50m rope, 8 bolt plates.

Recommended classics

Junket Pumper	18m	(24)	
Trix Roughly	12m	(26)	(Main Face)
Splitwave	18m	(23)	(Wave Wall)

MOUNT PIDDINGTON

One of the Blue Mountains' best crags. The compact rock of Mount Piddington specialises in easy natural leads, on some outstanding features. On the harder side of things there are some very thin faces and more testing steeper propositions, protected with bolts. Attractive views and convenient access all add to the popularity of this crag, particularly at weekends, making Piddington a good place to go if you're seeking a partner/belay slave for the day. The crag is also accessible on foot from Mount Victoria train station.

Geology: Sandstone

Number of climbs: 70

Grade of climbs: 8-27 (easy, middle)

Potential for new routes: No

Rock quality: Good

Protection: Bolts and natural pro

Length of climbs: 15-50m single, some 2 pitch

Predominant climbing style: Crack, slab, face and steep face

SPORT

Location and Access

Head north from Katoomba for 18km to the town of Mount Victoria. After a snaking left bend, just before the town centre, turn left onto Mount Piddington Road (signposted). If you pass the Imperial Hotel at a junction for Bell, you are now in town and have come too far. Half a kilometre leads to the top of Mount Piddington Road where a left turn is required. Follow this road for a few hundred metres and take the next right onto Carlisle Parade. Stay on this for a short distance downhill until it begins to swing right. Turn left here onto the dirt track to Mount Piddington. 300m down this is the top car park. It's best to walk from here.

Ten minutes' walk down a rough dirt road is the Hornes Point lookout. This is just above the right of the crag. Find a track leading off to the left for access to the cliffs down a rocky descent path (take care).

Camping and Supplies

There are no facilities at Mount Piddington, although camping is allowed. Some choose the top car park for their site. A far more pleasant stay is to camp in the Sundeck or Possum caves. These are found on either side of the alternative track through the bush to the cliffs (see map p126). Mount Victoria is fairly well facilitated with a hotel and café. For a prolonged stay at Mount Piddington getting well stocked at the large supermarkets of Sydney is advised.

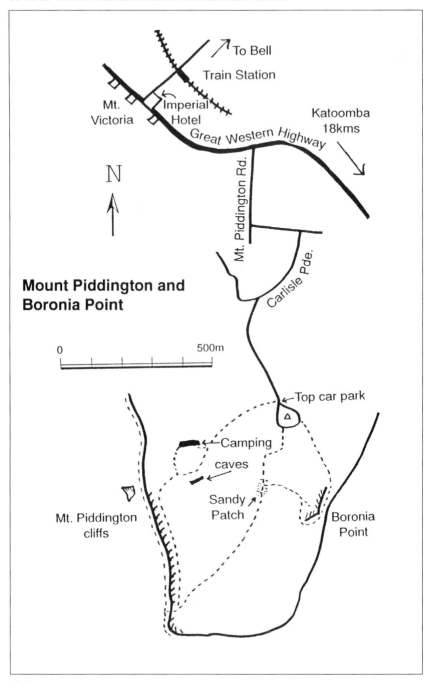

To Bell

Train Station

Mt.
Victoria

Imperial
Hotel

Katoomba
18kms

Great Western Highway

Mt. Piddington Rd.

N

Carlisle Pde.

**Mount Piddington and
Boronia Point**

0   500m

Top car park

Camping

caves

Sandy
Patch

Mt. Piddington
cliffs

Boronia
Point

What to take

A good rack of natural gear, friends and SLDCs are of particular use at Mount Piddington. For sport climbing, 6-8 bolt brackets. 1 x 50m rope. Drinking water, loo roll, sunscreen and hat.

Author's rating ***

Recommended classics

Eternity	26m	(19)
Tombstone Wall	25m	(15)
Flake Crack	34m	(17)
Flaming Youth	15m	(23)
Desirée	20m	(25)

BORONIA POINT

Another deservedly popular sport crag in the Blue Mountains. The east facing cliffs of Boronia Point make for steep and snatchy climbing. Overhanging rock helps shelter routes from the weather, perfect for summer, freezing in winter! Boronia Point as for Mount Piddington is accessible on foot from Mount Victoria train station.

Geology: Sandstone

Number of climbs: 20

Grade of climbs: 17-29 (middle grades)

Potential for new routes: No

Rock quality: Good

Protection: Bolts

Length of climbs: 10-35m single pitch

Predominant climbing style: Overhang, face

SPORT

Location and Access

See location and access for Mount Piddington for directions to the Mount Piddington top car park. From the car park walk down the rough dirt road, heading for Mount Piddington crag. After about 250m there is a sandy patch in the road. Take the small track on the left of the road here. Follow this short path to find the right-leading descent track at a cairn. This brings you to the base of Boronia Point after about 5 minutes' walk.

Camping and Supplies
See Mount Piddington.

What to take
Quickdraws and l large SLCD for the one route that requires it. Some bolt hangers are required for older routes. A rope bag to protect from ground dust.

Recommended classics

Cowboy Clip	10m	20
Silent Rage	15m	25
Sprouts Mexicaine	15m	24
Eureka	22m	23
Don't Believe the Tripe	30m	29

Author's rating *

MOUNT YORK

Mount York combines technical bolted face climbing with a bit of Australian history. The classic exhibition wall first climbed in the early 1970s is one of Australia's first bolted routes and a testpiece of its time. The easy access to some of the climbs is along Cox's Road, the original track made by the first explorers to cross the Blue Mountains. There is also a memorial at the car park to commemorate this.

Geology: Sandstone

Number of climbs: 50

Grade of climbs: 15-25

Potential for new routes: No

Rock quality: Good

Protection: Bolts, natural pro

Length of climbs: 15-35m single pitch

Predominant climbing style: Face

SPORT

Location and Access
Take the Great Northern Highway north for 19km from Katoomba to reach the right turning (signposted) for Mount York, 1km outside the town of Mount Victoria. Follow this road for 5km to the parking loop at the end. Both climbing areas, the 'sunny' and 'shady' sides (north and west faces of the Mt. York peninsula), are

---

Dave Allen leads The 80 Minute Hour (18), Cosmic County. Photo: Max Bretherton

Klaus Klein on the Ladder of Gloom (19), Berowra, Sydney *Photo Klaus Klein*
Klaus Klein hangs on It's About 22 (24), Ball's Head, Sydney *Photo Klaus Klein*

easily accessible through the many descent gullies from here, (5 minutes' walk, see map).

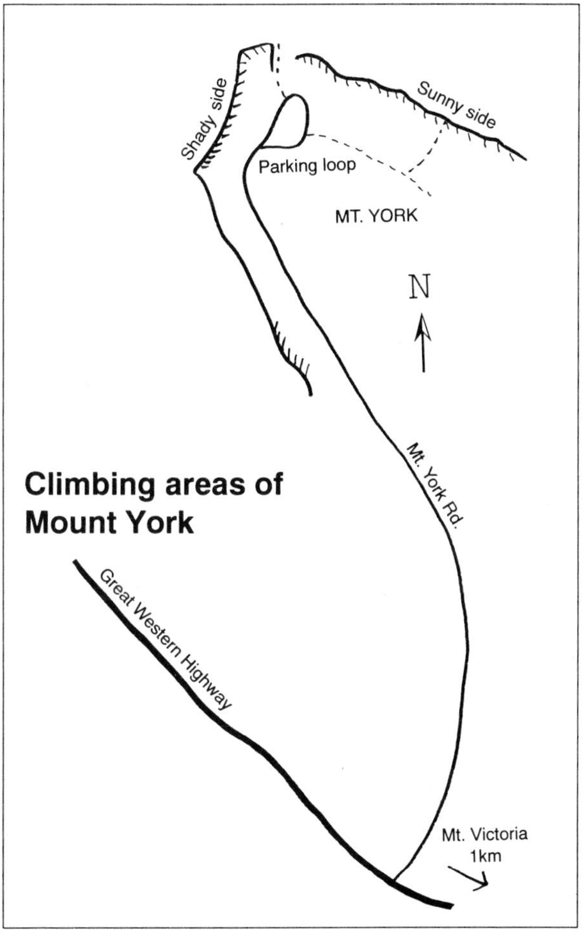

Camping and Supplies

Camping is allowed at Mount York. The shelters at the parking loop are popular sites. Toilets can be found at the Mitchell's picnic area, a short distance further north along the Great Western Highway, as there are no facilities at Mount York. Make a stop-off on the way to Mount York for supplies (eg. Katoomba). The nearest shops are 6km away in Mount Victoria.

What to take

A ground sheet to protect the rope, 12 bolt plates, natural pro, nuts, SLCD and friends, sunglasses, sunscreen and hat, drinking water.

Climbing areas of
Mount York

Author's rating *

Recommended classics

Exhibition Wall	30m	21
Ashes to Ashes	25m	25

COSMIC COUNTY

If only a short time is available in the Blue Mountains then the Cosmic County would have to be first choice (closely followed by Mount Piddington). Basically a

129

line of impressive sandstone blocks, creating a fine collection of extensive vertical walls, faces and arêtes, making this a deservedly popular crag. Compelling outlooks across the ravine, well protected climbs of good length and variety, all within 5 minutes of parking, where the best camping of the mountains can be found under the shelter of gum trees. It is a great place to be, where many an enjoyable day's climbing awaits.

Geology: Sandstone

Number of climbs: 100

Grade of climbs: 16-26

Potential for new routes: No

Rock quality: Excellent

Protection: Bolts, natural pro

Length of climbs: 15-100m single, few multi-pitch

Predominant climbing style: Face, arête

SPORT

Location and Access

From Katoomba, continue north along the Great Western Highway for 18km to Mount Victoria. Turn right at the Imperial Hotel (signposted) and follow this road for 11km to reach the T-junction of Chifley Road (40) at the small settlement of Bell. Turn left here. After approximately 10km look out for a left turning onto Petra Avenue, across from the zigzag railway turning. Turn left at the top of Petra Avenue. This road deteriorates to a dirt track after a short distance. Turn right at the end onto the start of the fire trails. A short but slow drive down this track arrives at a fiveway junction. Go straight across taking the second right (see map). Half a kilometre down this track turn left. This ends at the car park and camping area. Access to the cliffs is a short walk down the trail from the bottom of the car park.

Camping and Supplies

Probably the best camping of the Blue Mountains is available at Cosmic County. There are no facilities, but there is no charge and the pleasantly spacious area allows ample room for car side tents and fires (observe fire bans when applicable). There is also a water supply a few hundred metres away named the Kidney Bowl, an ideal set up for budget travellers in particular. Get well stocked and tanked for all required provisions, preferably in Sydney or at Katoomba, before arriving at Cosmic County as there are no shops within the area.

When to go

The cliffs of the county face west, therefore summer afternoons and winter mornings are out.

What to take

2 x 50m ropes for commonly long abseil. As many as 12 bolt plates for some routes. SLCDs and a selection of friends fit nicely in the typical cosmic breaks.

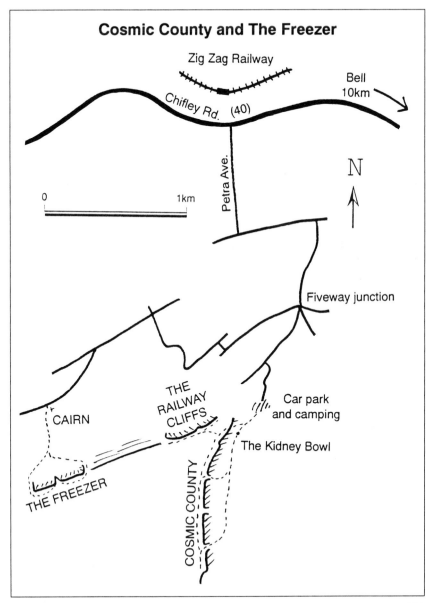

Cosmic County and The Freezer

Recommended classics

I must go Down to the Sea Again	100m	25	(The Railway Cliffs)
The Bells, the Bells	45m	21	(The Railway Cliffs)
I'd rather be Sailing	40m	19	
Walking Wounded	20m	23	
The 80 minute Hour	30m	18	
Barbarousa	40m	21	
Touchstone	30m	19	

Author's rating *

THE FREEZER

This authentic Australian sport crag offers long and steep single-pitch climbing. Fixed hangars and ring bolts are plenty on this upper section of yellow rock, called The Freezer.

Geology: Sandstone

Number of climbs: 20

Grade of climbs: 20-27

Potential for new routes: No

Rock quality: Sound

Protection: Bolts, fixed hangers

Length of climbs: 20-35m single pitch

Predominant climbing style: Overhang face

SPORT

Location and Access (see map p131)
See location and access for Cosmic County to reach the fiveway junction. Turn right here to follow a poor dirt road down over a ford. Continue up the winding road until cables can be seen above the track. Turn left here. 600m down this track, veering left at the fork leads to a pile of rocks (cairn). Park on the trackside here. Go down the walking track off the same side of the road as the cairn. Five minutes' trek finds the first descent path on the right of the crag. There is also a descent path further along on the left of the crag. Once at the base of the cliffs, the two sections of rock which make up The Freezer are connected by a hanging log and rope support rail. This crosses a narrow canyon below. Clip into the rope with a sling and carabiner attached to your harness when crossing the log, as a slip could be fatal or result in serious injury.

Camping and Supplies
Camping is not suitable at The Freezer. See 'Camping and supplies' for Cosmic County.

When to go
The Freezer faces east making it a good choice for summer climbing as it avoids the afternoon sun. The steep wall also offers good shelter in wet conditions.

What to take
1 x 50m rope, 13 quickdraws, drinking water, a muscular physique!

Useful information
Make sure you are well practised at lowering off a single ring bolt. This is essential for safety whilst climbing at The Freezer.

Author's rating *

TARANA

One of the few granite formations in New South Wales. Probably not worth the long journey from Sydney, but if you are passing through, a good place to stop for a pleasant afternoon's slab climbing. Tarana's climbs are not dissimilar to each other, which generally wrap up to be well protected balancing acts on good rock in a very pretty area.

Geology: Granite

Number of climbs: 100

Grade of climbs: 10-26 (middle grade)

Predominant climbing style: Slab

Rock quality: Sound

Protection: Bolts and natural pro

Length of climbs: 8-85m mostly single

Potential for new routes: No - by order of the NDWS Bathurst district

SPORT

Location and Access (see map p118)
The climbing at Tarana is in the Evans Crown Nature Reserve 160km west of Sydney. Leave Sydney via the Great Western Highway, driving up and over the Blue Mountains for 140km towards Lithgow. At a service station just before Lithgow, turn onto Rydal Road. Follow this, passing a lake on the right-hand side, up to a T-junction. Turn right here, then next left onto Tarana Road. 8km along

this poor road, turn left onto Honeysuckle Falls Road (signposted). Park 2km up this road by the Evans Crown Nature Reserve sign. The climbing can be found by crossing the fence stile then following the foot track, veering left at the boulders, to meet the first section of cliff after 10 minutes' walking.

Camping and Supplies
Camping is not allowed within the reserve. Several pubs in Lithgow offer accommodation. Tourist information centre at 285 Main Street, Lithgow: Tel (063) 51 2307.

Climate and when to go
Climbing at Tarana is a three season event from Sept to May. In summer this is a good alternative when the Blue Mountains are too hot as the cliffs lie in the afternoon shade.

What to take
Many routes at Tarana are purely bolted where bolt plates are required. Natural protection, particularly friends, will be of use on other routes. Long abseils are eliminated on most routes by descent tracks, making 1 x 50m rope adequate for climbing Tarana.

Recommended classics
Dr Marten's Boots   25m   21   (Deckout Buttress)

Useful information
For more information on climbing in the Evans Crown Nature Reserve contact National Parks and Wildlife Service, Bathurst District, 154 Russell Street, Bathurst, NSW 2795. Tel (063) 31 9777.

Guide to climbs
Evans Crown, Tarana, a Rock Guide by Mark Colyan (1990)
The Blue Mountains, a Guide to Selected Rock Climbs (including Tarana) by Michael Law (1994)

THE WARRUMBUNGLES
The Warrumbungles is the adventure climbing centre of New South Wales, holding the largest collection of 200m+ routes in the country. This captivating national park was one of the first climbing areas of Australia to be conquered. First ascents made in the early 1960s were often daring and heroic tasks, giving the cliffs a real feel of prestige. The climbing is set in verdant flora, amongst classic

Australian fauna, on outstanding rock spires and mountains. The 350m north face of Bluff Mountain is particularly stunning.

NB. Climbs in the Warrumbungles are often long and serious undertakings. Ascent, routefinding and retreat can be difficult. Experience in natural gear placement and routefinding are essential skills. Problems in routefinding are often referred to as 'The Warrumbungle factor'!

Geology: Sandstone

Number of climbs: 200

Grade of climbs: 4-23

Potential for new routes: Yes

Rock quality: Sound

Protection: Natural pro, few bolts

Length of climbs: 30-360m multi-pitch

Predominant climbing style: Long adventure climbing

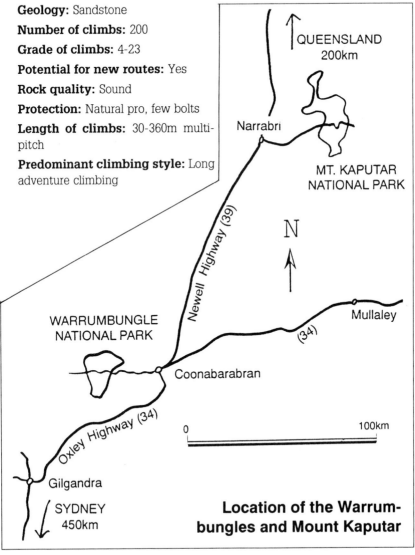

Location of the Warrumbungles and Mount Kaputar

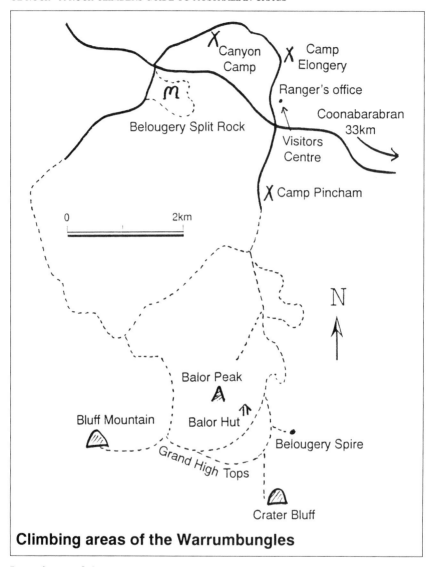

Climbing areas of the Warrumbungles

Location and Access

The Warrumbungle National Park is approximately 500km north-west of Sydney in central New South Wales, a good day's drive away. Head out of Sydney on the Great Western Highway. At 200km go north-west on the Mitchel Highway (32). A further 200km turn north at Dubbo onto the Newell Highway (39). Turn right at Gilgandra onto the Oxley Highway (34). This leads to the town of Coonabarabran. The National Park is 33km west of this town via a well signposted road.

On arrival at the Warrumbungles, park entrance and camping fees are payable at the ranger's office where a mandatory rock climbing permit can also be obtained free of charge.

The most popular climbing areas of Belougery Spire, Crater Bluff and Bluff Mountain are all within walking distance of the Balor Hut camping ground, which is $1^{1}/_{2}$ hours' walk from Camp Pincham, the nearest parking area to Balor Hut (see map).

Bluff Mountain is the furthest area of the three from the Balor Hut and is a good hour's walk away. Descent from the summits in most cases is by 50m abseil from chains to descent tracks.

Camping and Supplies

As previously mentioned camping is permitted within the National Park. The most popular site for climbers is at the Balor Hut, where drinking water is available from a water tank. For longer stays at the Warrumbungles a visit to the camping areas near the ranger's office may be required. Facilities there include toilets, wash basins, hot showers and a public telephone. Camping fees and park entrance fees are payable at the ranger's office.

Food and petrol are not available within the National Park. Filling up the tank and shopping bags at Coonabarabran is necessary before setting off for the park.

Climate and when to go

Spring (Sept-Nov) and autumn (Feb-Mar) are the best times to visit the Warrumbungles due to the moderate temperatures at these times. Year round climbing is possible, however, depending on how extreme the seasons are for any given year. In summer, temperatures can reach 40°C. (NB. Consult ranger as to bushfire danger in these conditions.) In winter nights often drop below freezing and an occasional drop of snow is not unheard of.

What to take

A full rack of wires, SLCDs and friends of all sizes, and a few bolt brackets. Double rack of wires for Bluff Mountain. Remember this is adventure climbing where routes are uncommonly direct lines, therefore plenty of 60cm slings to extend runners to minimise rope drop area required. 2 x 50m ropes for double rope leading and 50m abseils. Helmets are standard equipment in the Warrumbungles. Head torches should be taken on long routes, in case of a benighting! Firewood, which is not available in the park.

Recommended classics

Vertigo	78m	10	(Belougery Spire)
Lieban	260m	17	(Crater Bluff)
Cornerstone Rib Direct	190m	14	(Crater Bluff)

137

Bastion Buttress	240m	13	(Bluff Mountain)
Flight of the Phoenix	330m	18	(Bluff Mountain)
Ginsberg	332m	19	(Bluff Mountain)

Useful information

Ranger's office (068) 25 4364, after hours (068) 25 4376.

Warrumbungle National Park, PO Box 39, Coonabarabran, NSW 2357.

Some of the routes in the Warrumbungles were put up 30 years ago and piton runners were used. Many of these are now badly corroded and should be treated with caution.

Author's rating ***

Guide to climbs

A Climber's Guide to the Warrumbungles by Mark Colyvan (1995) (available at visitor's centre)

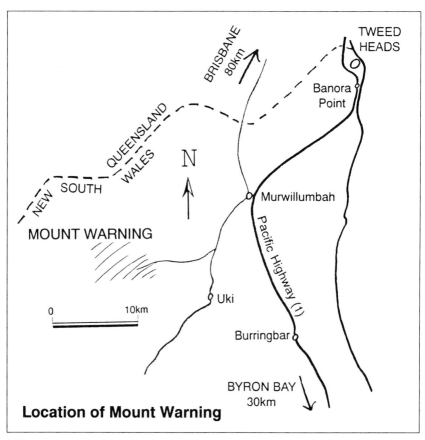

Location of Mount Warning

MOUNT WARNING

The very far north-east of NSW is dominated by the impressive 1100m cone of Mount Warning. This mountain has just one climb, graded 24M1 with 15 pitches over 568m: The Lost Boys on the Wollumbin Shield (north face) is a bit of a world beater! The climbing is very isolated on compact basalt involving steep blank walls and slabs with roofs every 50-100m. A huge effort has gone into this massive undertaking as there are some 98 bolts (31 of which are belay anchors) throughout the climb.

Warning: The Lost Boys is a very difficult and serious venture. Experience in big wall climbing is essential, as is a high level of fitness, as pitches are typically long, thin and very sustained. EXPERIENCED CLIMBERS ONLY.

Location and Access

The Mount Warning National Park is located 15km west and south of Murwillumbah, a town close to the coast and Queensland border. Drive south from the town heading for Uki, Nimbin and Lismore. A few kms before Uki, turn right onto the 6km Mount Warning approach road. To access the climb follow the tourist track up the east face to the west summit. This begins through the enchanting rainforest at the base of the mountain, then leads to the zigzag of the east face. The walk from the car park takes between 2 and 4 hours (depending on fitness) to reach the summit. From the west summit, a short steep descent through grass trees leads to the top bivvy area, marked by a cairn. There are also three eucalyptus trees for the first abseil station over the 400m drop. (See map for more details about the climb.) A series of 10 abseils reaches the base of the cliff from here. Walk a few hundred metres to the left at the base of the cliff to find the start of the climb marked by a cairn.

Camping and supplies

Camping is not allowed within the Mount Warning NP. Camping is available at the Wollumbin Refuge Caravan Park situated on the Mount Warning approach road. Murwillumbah is a good source for supplies.

Climate and when to go

If you are on the summit at daybreak, you'll be the first person on mainland Australia to see the sun that day. Climbing in the summer gets a little too hot and uncomfortable as the face is well exposed to the sun. Spring and autumn offer the best conditions.

What to take

2 or 3 days' food and water, 2 or 3 x 50m ropes, slings and quickdraws, sun cream and shades, bivvy bags, sleeping bags and warm clothing, a full rack of wires and a full set of SLCDs.

Useful information

The series of abseils required to reach the base of the climb from the summit takes about 2½ hours to complete. Most climbers choose to reach the summit by evening and camp at the top bivvy in order to make an early start on the abseils and spend the following 2 days completing the climb. NB. The Lost Boys has never been done in one continuous ascent.

Author's rating *

MOUNT KAPUTAR

Considering the quality and variety of climbing that is available within this National Park, it is little talked about and surprisingly unpopular. This is probably due to its location, although only a further 100km north of the Warrumbungles. Those who do venture to Mount Kaputar will be well rewarded, with some considerably good climbing. A cliff of particular note is The Governor offering some excellent middle grade multi-pitches. Route location is also easy as many climbs are initialled.

Geology: Trachyte (light coloured, rough, volcanic)

Number of climbs: 350

Grade of climbs: 3-26

Potential for new routes: Yes

Rock quality: Sound

Protection: Natural pro and bolts

Length of climbs: 10-140m single and multi-pitch

Predominant climbing style: All styles

Location and Access

Mount Kaputar National Park is approximately 600km north-west of Sydney, 200km south of the Queensland border. See location and access for Warrumbungle for directions to the town of Connabarabran from Sydney. Drive 118km north on the Newell Highway (39) from Connabarabran to the town of Narrabri. 50km east of Narrabri is the National Park. Turn right at the town and follow the signs up the steep gravel road.

Access to most cliffs varies between 10 and 30 minutes' walking from parking on the roadside. The best climbing and most popular cliff is The Governor. From The Governor car park follow the track, then down a ladder and gully to arrive in 10 minutes at the base of the right-hand end of the cliff. Another popular area, Euglah Rock, holds some excellent 1 and 2 pitch hauls. This is a 20 minute walk

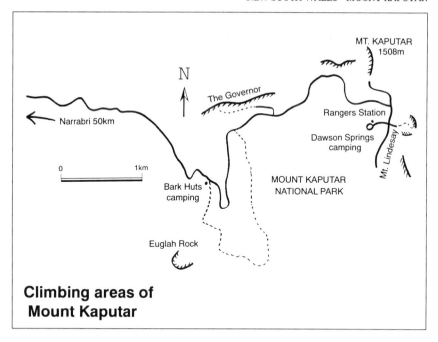

Climbing areas of
Mount Kaputar

along the uphill track near the Bark Huts camping area. Use 2 x 50m ropes to abseil from the trees on the cliff tops. Mount Lindesay and Mount Kaputar are also good climbing areas.

Camping and Supplies
There are two camping areas at Mount Kaputar National Park, the Bark Huts and Dawson Springs sites, where facilities include water, hot showers, toilets and fire places. Fees apply. Food and fuel is not available within the National Park. The town of Narrabri makes an excellent stop to purchase such items.

Climate and when to go
The months between Sept and May have conditions best suited for climbing. An elevation of 1500m, however, does not allow climbing during the winter, as the park will often be snow covered with daytime temperatures of only a few degrees.

What to take
A rack of natural protection, nuts and small wires in particular, 8 bolt brackets, 2 x 50m ropes.

Recommended classics

Iconoclast	80m	20	(The Governor)
Great Barrier Roof	67m	23	(The Governor)
The Millionaire Touch	103m	24	(The Governor)
Insidious	30m	14	(Euglah Rock)
Edge effects	40m	23	(Euglah Rock)
Yummilkins	33m	17	(Euglah Rock)

Useful information

The park rangers would like to be informed either prior to or on arrival at Mount Kaputar of all climbing trips. They can also give information about the park - maps, details on climbing areas and new routes.

Take great care at the Mount Kaputar National Park to make minimum impact during your stay. Particularly, respect should be shown towards the cliffs and wildlife on them, as the park gives habitat to many rare species.

Contact the ranger: PO Box 72, Narrabri, NSW 2390

National Park Tel (067) 92 1147

Ranger Tel (067) 92 2788 or 92 1354

Author's rating *

Guide to climbs

Kaputar, a Rock Guide by Mark Colyon (1993)

CLIMBING AROUND SYDNEY

Sydney, the city of sandstone, is home to Australia's best suburban climbing. These well located sport crags are found as little as 15 minutes from the city centre. Exciting sea cliffs, high escarpments, airy headlands, roofs, caves and Australia's best bouldering all add to the variety of natural rock formations to be discovered when climbing around Sydney.

Camping and supplies
Camping is not permitted at any of Sydney's crags, nor are there campsites within the area. However, there are plenty of cheap hostels around, as Sydney is a popular crossroads for thousands of travellers each year. Areas of concern include King's Cross, Glebe, Bondi Beach, Coogeebeach and on the north shore Neutral Bay and Manly.

Sydney is Australia's shopping capital, so finding a store to suit your daily or even yearly requirements will not be a problem here. If stocking up for a long trip, try the country's largest growing supermarket at Neutral Bay.

Climate and when to go
Of the four major Australian cities, Sydney has the highest annual rainfall, so be prepared for a good soaking at any time of year. When this does occur, the caves of West Lindfield are a sheltered option.

Year round climbing is possible at all Sydney's crags, but some destinations are best suited for different conditions. Summers are hot. The highest recorded temperature in 1995 was a staggering 45°C! In this event, cooler outings include the north Narrabeen slabs, Kalkari and Middle Cove. Whereas winter can have very pleasant conditions, if temperatures do dip below the comfort zone, Berowra, Barrenjoey's west side and south Narrabeen are wise selections.

Useful information
For more information about climbing around Sydney contact Mountain Designs, 499 Kent Street, Sydney. Tel (02) 267 8238.

Guide to climbs
Sydney and the Sea Cliffs a Rock Guide by Mike Law (1991)

BEROWRA
This great little cliff, with lovely views across the Madgamarra Nature Reserve, offers bolt protected face climbing, usually on pockets or thin edges. The rock is in direct sunlight making Berowra perfect for winter climbing. Care should be taken after heavy rainfall, as overflow from the top soil can make holds dirty.

143

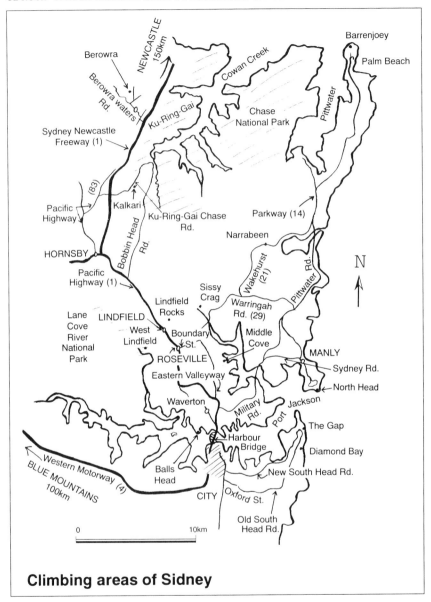

Climbing areas of Sidney

Geology: Sandstone

Number of climbs: 40

Grade of climbs: 16-25

Predominant climbing style: Face

Rock quality: Good, but often dirty

Protection: Bolts, some natural pro

Length of climbs: 10-15m single pitch

Potential for new routes: No

SPORT

Location and Access

From the city cross the Harbour bridge, continue north along the freeway and the Pacific Highway. After 24km turn right onto the Sydney/Newcastle Freeway (1). 10km along this turn off for Berowra (signposted). At the top of the slipway turn left, then right at the T-junction back onto the Pacific Highway. In a few hundred metres turn left at the lights down Berowra Waters Road. At the first roundabout turn right and then right at the next roundabout, a short distance after the first one. Take the second left along this road onto Wide View Road, drive to and park at the end of this road (45 minutes' drive).

To access the cliffs, find the foot track leading through the bushes on the left of the road. Two minutes' walking will present the cliff top. There are descent tracks at both ends of the cliff.

What to take

1 x 50m rope, 5 bolt plates, drinking water, sun hat and screen. A belay helmet as there are many loose stones on the cliff top.

Author's rating *

Recommended classics

Ladder of Gloom	12m	19
Palm Sunday	15m	21
Alison	12m	25
Looks Poxable	15m	21

KALKARI

Not as impressive or extensive as other Sydney greats. Nonetheless, being well hidden amongst the bush of Ku-ring-gai Chase National Park, the steep and generally hard shaded climbs of Kalkari offer a pleasant change for an afternoon, particularly in summer.

145

Geology: Sandstone

Number of climbs: 15

Grade of climbs: 19-26

Predominant climbing style: Steep face roof

Rock quality: Fair

Protection: Bolts, a few natural pro

Length of climbs: 10-25m single pitch

Potential for new routes: Yes, for higher grades

SPORT

Location and Access (see map p144)

From the city, cross the Harbour bridge and continue for 30km on the freeway and the Pacific Highway (1), turning right at Hornsby to stay on the Pacific Highway (83). Approximately 6kms from Hornsby turn right onto the Ku-ring-gai Chase Road. A few km along this road leads to the Kalkari 'visitor centre' sign. If you are parked on the left, cross the road and follow a vague track through the scrub for about 50m until a descent track is found at the right-hand side of the cliff.

What to take

1 x 50m rope, drinking water, 9 bolt plates.

Recommended classics

The American Way	12m	21
Rushmore	15m	26
Led Zep 78	20m	26

NARRABEEN

The Narrabeen cliffs are serenely set and well camouflaged on the vegetated banks of Wakehurst Parkway. The two climbing areas not only physically oppose each other, they also offer contrasting styles of climbing. North of the road are the Narrabeen Slabs, while on the south is Narrabeen Steepside, both being self-evident from their names.

Geology: Sandstone

Number of climbs: 50

Grade of climbs: 15-27

Potential for new routes: Yes

Rock quality: Sound

Protection: Bolts, natural pro

Length of climbs: 5-20m single pitch

Predominant climbing style: Overhang, face, slab

SPORT

Location and Access

The two climbing areas of Narrabeen can be found opposite each other on Wakehurst Parkway, 20km north of Sydney. Leave the city north over the Harbour bridge following the freeway and Pacific Highway to the suburb of Roseville. Turn right here at the traffic lights down Boundary Street towards French Forest (signposted). A couple of kms of this straight road lead to a T-junction. Turn left here onto Warringah Road (29). Approximately 6km along this road is a fitness camp. At this point turn around and drive back down Wakehurst Parkway (south). 500m along the road south of the fitness camp on the right-hand side is a metal gate. Park on the roadside here for the Narrabeen Slabs. A further 500m south along Wakehurst Parkway is a lay-by on the left. Park here for Narrabeen Steepside.

Hop over the gate to find the Narrabeen Slabs a few minutes' walk up a foot track to the right. Narrabeen Steepside is a short walk from the lay-by to the cliffs. Follow an unclear track on the left (south) of the road.

What to take

1 x 50m rope, drinking water, 6 bolt plates, sunscreen on the steepside. Friends useful for naturally protected routes.

Recommended classics

Big Tick	15m	26	(Steepside)
Tilt	15m	22	(Steepside)
Common Origin	15m	16	(Slabs)
Technical Short Talk	16m	18	(Slabs)

BARRENJOEY AND PALM BEACH

The rock of Barrenjoey Head has good and varied single pitch climbing. Great views of the north and south coastline add hints of exposure in a general feeling of safety. This is a popular weekend area for water skiers, jet bikers, surfers, sunbathers and climbers alike, who all attribute to the Palm Beach sporting environment.

Geology: Sandstone

Number of climbs: 150

Grade of climbs: 5-25

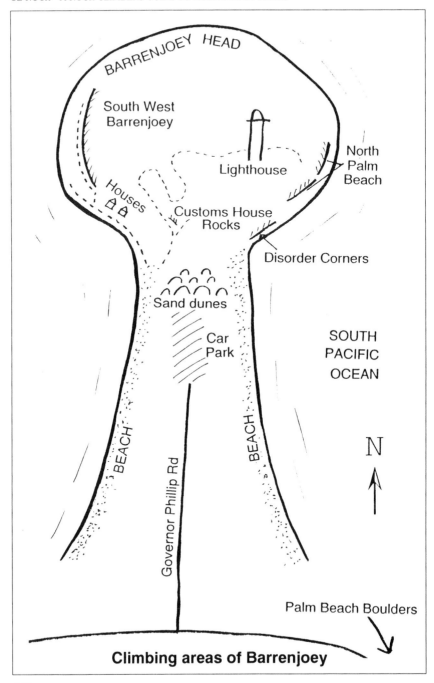

Climbing areas of Barrenjoey

Potential for new routes: No

Rock quality: Sound

Protection: Bolt, natural pro

Length of climbs: 5-25m single pitch

Predominant climbing style: All styles

SPORT

Location and Access
Barrenjoey is situated on the end of a northerly headland between South Pacific and Pittwater, just over an hour's drive from the city. Once over the Harbour bridge, take the second exit from the freeway for Neutral Bay, turning right at the top of the sliproad towards Neutral Bay along Military Road. Stay on this road for approximately 30km (change into Spit Road then Pittwater Road) (stay on Highway 14). Follow the road tending right after 25km towards Palm Beach (signposted). When as close to Barrenjoey headland as possible, before the road turns south down the ocean side, turn left along Governor Phillip Road, parking at the end of this in the sandy area.

The five climbing areas of Barrenjoey Head are 10-20 minutes' walk from the car park and are accessed as follows. The most popular area is the south-west area. From the car park walk left of the sand dunes, along the rocky shore, to find the track up to the cliffs next to two adjacent houses. The lighthouse track wall is a few hundred metres on the right up the lighthouse track. Further along the track is a signpost for the old Customs House site. Just after this is a right branching track leading to the Customs House Rocks. At the top of the lighthouse track, trails behind the lighthouse lead down to the North Palm Beach crags. Back at sea level, go right past the sand dunes from the car park along the beach and scree slope to find the Disorder Corners cliffs.

What to take
1 x 50m rope, hat, sunscreen and shades, standard rack of natural protection, 8 bolt plates.

Author's rating *

Recommended classics
Crack of Dawn	20m	15	(South-west)
Liquid Insanity	20m	18	(South-west)
Pulse of Fools	12m	25	(South-west)
Space Vampires	15m	18	(North)
The Holy Hour	15m	8	(North)

PALM BEACH

For a selection of excellent thin facey bouldering problems and a pumpy roof traverse, check out the two adjacent chunks of rock on the Palm Beach itself.

SYDNEY'S SEA CLIFFS

The following areas are Sydney's most popular coastal walls. However, proceed with the utmost caution. Although the crags have impressive architecture, providing some gripping exposure, the rock is often sandy and of poor quality. The sea cliffs are recommended for the experienced only. It is not unusual for a straightforward sport route to turn into an afternoon's epic! Apply wise judgement when using fixed protection as some bolts are corroded and should not be trusted. That aside, there are a few gems that are not to be missed if you are in the area. Sydney's longest and most exciting climbs (waves crashing below, the wind gusting in your ears) can be found on the sea cliffs.

NORTH HEAD

Geology: Sandstone

Number of climbs: 35

Grade of climbs: 16-23

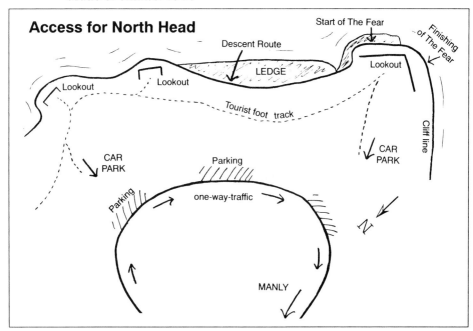

Potential for new routes: No

Rock quality: Fair

Protection: Natural pro and some bolts

Length of climbs: 10-60m single & multi-pitch

Predominant climbing style: Arêtes, corners, roofs, cracks

Location and Access

Take the second exit from the freeway over the Harbour bridge and follow the signs for Manly. On arrival at Manly (30 minutes from the city) drive through the town on the ferry wharf side (opposite the beach side). Continue up the hill following the tourist signs to the North Head lookout. Parking is available at the lookout.

To access the climbs find the fisherman's descent over the fence between the 2nd and 3rd lookouts (see map). The descent involves downclimbing 40m of sea weathered ropes, ladders, manufactured holds and iron bars. It is a precarious event and roping up is well advised. Routes to the left of the descent are along a ledge 10m from the ground. Complete the descent down a ladder to the ground for routes to the right.

What to take

1 x 50m rope; rack of friends; 10 bolt plates

Author's rating *

Recommended classics

The Fear	47m	17	(Sydney's most famous and notorious climb)
The Bolt Ladder	35m	20	

THE GAP/WATSONS BAY

Geology: Sandstone
Number of climbs: 20
Grade of climbs: 17-28
Potential for new routes: No
Rock quality: Sound
Protection: Natural pro and bolts
Length of climbs: 10-95m single & multi-pitch
Predominant climbing style: Overhanging

Location and Access (see map p144)

From the city, head east following signs to Double Bay to join New South Head Road (76). This road will take you to the tourists' car park for the Watsons Bay lookout (15 minutes' drive from the city). To access the climbs of the Mainwall abseil off the large triangular block just left of the main lookout. To reach the hardman's Duelling Biceps area walk about 250m south of the main lookout, then jump over the fence and scramble down to the south end of the slabs. There is a 3 bolt abseil point here. Rap in from this point (35m).

Leaving abseil ropes in place and taking jumars or prusik loops is strongly advised, as this is the only means of escape in the event of a failed route attempt.

What to take

3 x 50m ropes (2 for fixed abseil), rack of natural gear, friends in particular. 10 bolt plates, jumars and prusik loops.

Recommended classics

Cruise of Bruise	42m	20	(Mainwall)
Duelling Biceps	40m	23	(Duelling Biceps area)
Boyzone	95m	23	(Duelling Biceps area)

DIAMOND BAY

Geology: Sandstone

Number of climbs: 30

Grade of climbs: 16-26

Potential for new routes: No

Rock quality: Fair

Protection: Bolts & natural pro

Length of climbs: 10-35m single pitch

Predominant climbing style: Face

SPORT

Location and Access (see map p144)

Head east from the city on Oxford Street leading to Old South Head Road towards Watsons Bay. Look out for the turning of Diamond Bay Road after approximately 5km. Park at the end of this. The south gully is Diamond Bay and the cliffs can be accessed via a line of holds and ladders. (Be careful.)

What to take

2 x 50m ropes for the 35m route (1 x 50m is good for everything else), bolt plates, natural gear, particularly friends.

Recommended classics

Absolute Bosch	35m	23
What the Neighbours Think	18m	23
Ordeal by Fire	18m	25

BALL'S HEAD

This area had been included in this guidebook not for any great quality, length of climbing or indeed any notable formation. No, Ball's Head hosts the ultimate tourist's climbing photo. As the leader swings out through the pretty good roof climb over the water of Port Jackson, the photo is set. Legs and quickdraws dangle against the backing of Sydney's most famous landmark, the Harbour bridge!

Geology: Sandstone

Number of climbs: 10

Grade of climbs: 14-26

Potential for new routes: No

Rock quality: Sound

Protection: Bolts

Length of climbs: 10-15m single pitch

Predominant climbing style: Roof

SPORT

Location and Access (see map p144)

Ball's Head is located on the banks of Port Jackson to the north-west of the Harbour bridge. A short walk south from Waverton train station finds the car park. Walk down dirt tracks below this to find the cave by the water.

What to take

1 x 50m rope, 5 bolt plates, your camera!

Recommended classics

| It's About 22 | 15m | 24 |

MIDDLE COVE

Middle Cove is the essence of suburban climbing. The rocks are just a couple of hundred metres from your front door. Apparently nestled in parkland, the top of the 10m pebble reveals the network of surrounding streets and avenues. The cliffs are of no significance, however it's not a bad place to squeeze a bit in after work with only an hour's daylight to spare. Also lies in the shade, making Middle Cove good for summer.

Geology: Sandstone

Number of climbs: 14

Grade of climbs: 11-26

Potential for new routes: No

Rock quality: Fair

Protection: Bolts and natural gear

Length of climbs: 6-10m single pitch

Predominant climbing style: All styles (except roof)

Location and Access (see map p144)

Located in Harold Reid Reserve, off Rembrandt Drive, approximately 10km north of the city, close to the suburb of Castlecrag. If you park in the reserve make sure you're out by 5.30pm, as the gates close at this time. The rocks are a few hundred metres up the road from the entrance on the left.

What to take

1 x 50m rope, 4 bolt plates, friends and wires.

Recommended classics

Unnameable Arête   9m   21

BOULDERING IN SYDNEY
LINDFIELD ROCKS

Regarded by some as one of Australia's best bouldering areas. This ideal congregation of brilliant rocks has something for everyone. Being well situated with problems varying from butter knife faces to pumpy roofs (including all the cracks, slabs, overhangs and blasting dynos you could ask for), Lindfield Rocks is a justly popular spot. It's an excellent place to meet the local enthusiast and perhaps organise trips further afield. If you are interested in testing roof movements ask around for the Pipedreams Cave. In summary, whatever your climbing interests, there's many a fine hour's bouldering to be had at Lindfield Rocks.

Location and access

A 20 minute train ride or drive north of the city along the Pacific Highway will find the suburb of Lindfield. Once in the town pass the post office on the left, over a pedestrian crossing, then turn right at the traffic lights by the supermarket. Follow the short road under the bridge to turn right at the T-junction. 150m up this road

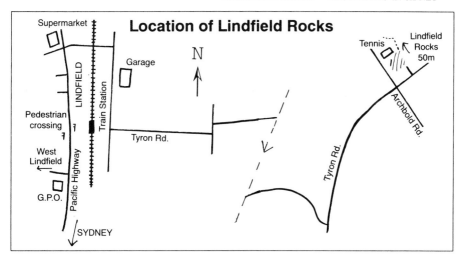

take the left turning into Tyron Road across from the train station. After 1km including a road crossing, steep hill and a tight left bend, Tyron Road meets Archbold Road. Cross over this, taking the first left after the lights. Park by the tennis courts and toilets (15 minutes' walk from the train station). Walk down the track to the right of the tennis courts, branching left down the staircase to find the rocks in 30 seconds.

Author's rating **

SISSY CRAG

Unlike the name suggests, this is no place for any cowardly behaviour! A more apt name would be 'Damned hard problems crag'! Lots of steep rock with lots of great moves. The array of toughies start at around V4 and go up from there - enough to keep any hardman entertained.

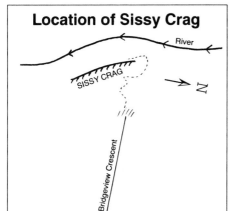

Location and Access

Sissy Crag is approximately 12km north of the city. Follow the Pacific Highway to the suburb of Roseville. Turn right here onto Boundary Street. Follow this to its end, to turn left onto Warringah Road. Drive north from here across the Roseville bridge towards Brookvale and Manly. After crossing the bridge take the second left, Ryrie Avenue, and then the next left, Bridgeview Crescent. Park at the end of Bridgeview Crescent. A short walk down the track at the end of the road between some small ferns will bring you to the left of the crag.

WEST LINDFIELD

If you are in Sydney long enough to get bored of Lindfield Rocks and Sissy Crag, West Lindfield is a good alternative and worthy of a visit in its own right. A recently discovered area, The Block, has some thin, reachy and powerful problems, whereas the well known caves by the creek have a good low level traverse, The Big Pump and an excellent body stretching sequence of roof moves in the lower cave.

Location and Access
As for Lindfield Rocks head north along the Pacific Highway to the suburb of

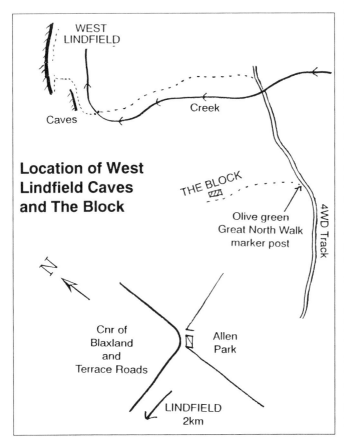

Lindfield. This time take the left turn immed-iately after the post office down Beaconsfield Parade, turning right at the end of it. Park on the roadside on the corner of Blax-land and Terr-ace Roads by the entrance to Allen Park. Walk straight across the grass veer-ing slightly left to a 4 wheel drive dirt track. For The Block take the first narrow track on the left, marked by an olive green 'Great North Walk'

marker post. A couple of minutes' walking under large roofs leads to the obvious block on the right of the track. To reach West Lindfield proper regain the 4 wheel drive track, branching left at the bottom to walk alongside Lane Cove River. When the track crosses the water by stepping stones, look up and right to see the caves.

NOWRA

Climb hard. Climb harder! If you must climb hard today, look no further. The 30 or so climbing areas of Nowra together make Australia's number one sport climbing destination. The grease cave at Thompson's Point has the largest concentration of hard climbs per m^2 in the southern hemisphere and South Central now holds Australia's equally hardest climb! A third of all the climbs at Nowra are graded 24 plus. However it is not only the grades that are high, the number of quality, mega classics is also well above the norm. Access is a breeze for these waterside locations which any sporting climber would be a fool to miss.

Geology: Sandstone

Number of climbs: 300

Grade of climbs: 7-32 (75% 20+)

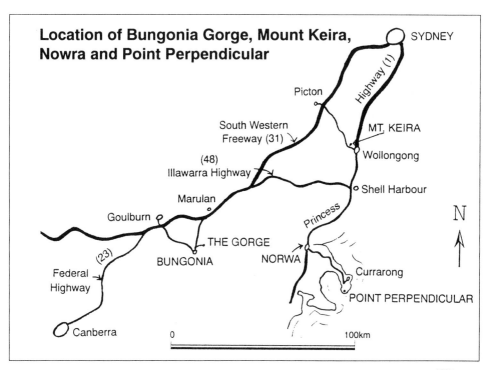

Location of Bungonia Gorge, Mount Keira, Nowra and Point Perpendicular

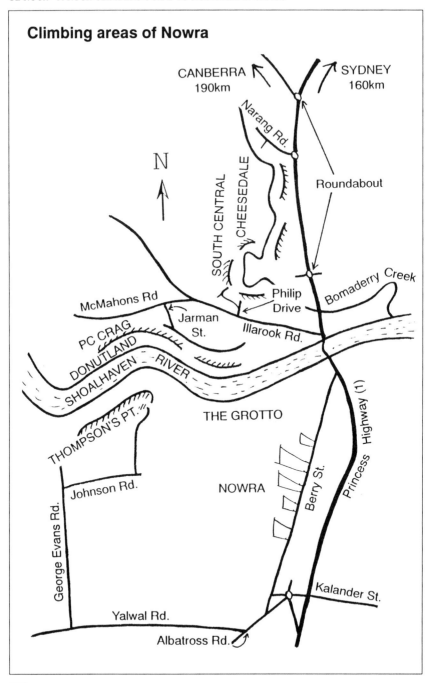

Climbing areas of Nowra

Predominant climbing style: Overhangs

Rock quality: Excellent

Protection: Bolts, few natural pro

Length of climbs: 5-35m single pitch

Potential for new routes: Yes, for very hard climbs

SPORT

Location and Access

The town of Nowra, set in attractive coastal lands, is 160km south of Sydney (about 2 hours' drive). Leave the city to the south past the airport on the Princess Highway. This connects to the Southern Freeway. Stay with this road, bypassing Wollongong and Shell Harbour to arrive at the town of Nowra 43km after Kiama. The four most extensive climbing areas are all a short drive from the town centre.

To access the climbing of the most popular area, Thompson's Point, use the map to find the parking area at the end of the dirt track. Walk towards the river and three power poles. A track leads off to the right through scrub. A short distance along this there are a couple of ledges to jump down, then a narrow descent gully on the left. The gully ends at the left (east) side of the Thompson's Point cliffline.

Camping and supplies

Camping is not permitted at any climbing areas at Nowra. Please respect this rule, leaving cliffs open for all. There are several campsites in the Nowra region, one of the nearest being Nowra Animal Park across from Thompson's Point, Tel (044) 213 949. Or the Shoalhaven Caravan Village on Terrace Road, Tel (044) 230 770. Nowra can be a busy little town with all the usual commercial and produce outlets to meet most climbers' needs (eg. bakery, fast food, café, off-licence, etc.).

Climate and when to go

Nowra's climate is renowned for being warm and then hot. Autumn, winter and spring are all possibilities. The best time to go is in winter when the Blue Mountains and places of similar altitude are too cold. The north facing rock of Thompson's Point is particularly good at this time, where on a sunny day you'll still be getting your T shirt off to mop your brow. On days of less favourable conditions the cliffs of South Central are an option as they remain sheltered in the rain. Climbing at Nowra during summer is not recommended. Soaring temperatures and the difficulty of the climbs could seriously damage your health (not to mention your ego!).

What to take

The majority of climbs are protected with fixed hangers and abseil chains or ring

159

and U bolts, so don't come to Nowra to test your sparkling new set of rocks. A few bolt plates will come in handy on some routes, but in the main 12 quickdraws, a rope and a pair of emergency biceps will do the job!

Recommended classics

Vanderholics	25m	19	(Thompson's Point)
Stone Roses	25m	26	(Thompson's Point)
Killer Boas	10m	22	(Thompson's Point)
Je Baise Ma Fraigne	10m	20	(Thompson's Point)
Muscle Hustler	35m	26	(Thompson's Point)
Slip Slap Slop	10m	30	(Thompson's Point)
Sexy is the Word	10m	31	(Thompson's Point)
Pulling on the Porcelain	12m	23	(Thompson's Point)
Black Beddy	8m	23	(Thompson's Point)
Conehead and the			
Barbiturates	15m	22	(The Grotto)
Slats and Udders	10m	22	(The Grotto)
Ain't No Sunshine			
when he's Gone	15m	28	(South Central)
Crime is Art	10m	23	(South Central)
Evil Dick	10m	22	(Bomaderry Creek)
Pussy Box Sores	10m	21	(Bomaderry Creek)

Useful information

National Parks office, 24 Berry street, Nowra. Tel (044) 21 9969.

Author's rating ***

Guide to climbs

Rockclimber's Guide to Nowra and Wollongong edited by Rod Young (1994)

NB. The climbing at Nowra continues to develop. Many projects are on the go and still await first ascents. A bit of tape or ribbon on the first or second bolt denotes a project route. Respect somebody else's planning, cleaning and bolting effort by leaving these routes alone, so the first ascent is bagged by the entitled person.

BUNGONIA GORGE

This beautiful gorge is Australia's big wall experience. Not quite the El Cap, but some fine and extensive multi-pitch routes all the same. A recently developed crag offering traditional adventure climbing, fully protected by natural gear of the more modern style of long ascents, where crux sections, belay stations and sometimes entire pitches are bolt protected, making retreat a far less hazardous act. The walls of Bungonia have literally repelled many a strong leader, mainly due to the difficulty of the routes, the majority being graded in the early 20s.

Geology: Limestone

Number of climbs: 60

Grade of climbs: 16-26 (most 20)

Potential for new routes: Yes

Rock quality: Good

Protection: Bolts and natural pro

Length of climbs: 15-365m 50% multi-pitch

Predominant climbing style: Corner, scoops, cracks, ledges, roofs, faces

Location and Access

Bungonia Gorge lies 30km east of the Goulburn, just off the South Western Freeway, 2½ hours' drive south of Sydney and 1½ hours' drive north of Canberra. Pick up the South Western Motorway (5) from Sydney. Stay with this for 190km to turn left just past the town of Marulan, heading south towards the town of Bungonia. Find the short signposted road to the gorge from the town. Park just before the lookout on the right in the David Reid car park. To access the main climbing area, the north and south faces of the gorge, take the Red Efflux track marked by red squares on trees (20 minutes' walk). For the few single pitch 'sport' climbs that exist at the gorge, rap in to double bolt belays from the double ring bolts found near the Cooee Point lookout. There is also an excellent cliff for beginners, founded by the Sydney Rockclimbers Club, below the Adams lookout.

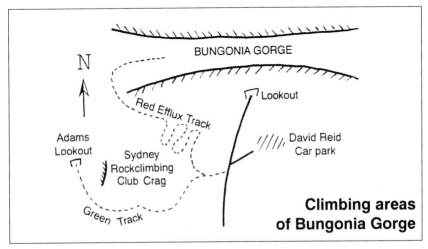

Camping and Supplies

Camping is not permitted within the gorge, however there is an excellent camping area within Bungonia's recreation area. Facilities include fire places, toilets and showers. For more information Tel (048) 484 277. The most economical option for supplies is Goulburn, 28km to the west.

Climate and when to go

Climbing is perennial at Bungonia Gorge. It's not that the gorge's climate does not have extremes. It's simply a matter of choosing the right side to suit the conditions. When it's hot, climb in the shade of the North Wall and at cooler times catch the sun all day on the South Wall.

What to take

2 x 50m ropes, plenty of slings, helmets strongly advised for climbing at Bungonia Gorge, an extensive rack of natural pro including double sets of friends and 2 sets of nuts and RPs.

Recommended classics

Critical Mass	85m	24	(North West End Wall)
Strangeness and Charm	160m	22	(North West End Wall)
Jewel Box	150m	23	(North West End Wall)
Red Supergiant	365m	20	(South Wall)
Siblings of the Sun	235m	26	(South Wall)
Albino	240m	24	(South Wall)

Useful information

For more information on Bungonia state recreation area Tel (048) 484 277. Maps of all walking tracks and lookouts at the gorge are available from the ranger's station.

Author's rating *

Guide to climbs

Strangeness and Charm, Rock Climbing in Bungonia Gorge edited by Mike Law-Smith

MOUNT KEIRA (WOLLONGONG)

A high escarpment on quite a dramatic uprising, overlooking Wollongong and the surrounding rainforest and coastal area. If the tendon ripping strains of Nowra aren't quite your scene, Mount Keira is a pleasant and contrasting option. Popular with beginners, The Big K has a good selection of climbing over a solid span of grades. Good protection on natural lines and well bolted sport routes are both at hand. Also look out for bouldering on the west face and at Pox Crag (east side of the north face).

Geology: Sandstone

Number of climbs: 180

Grade of climbs: 6-26

Potential for new routes: No

Rock quality: Sound

Protection: Bolts, natural pro

Length of climbs: 5-50m single - 3 pitch

Predominant climbing style: Face, arête, crack

SPORT

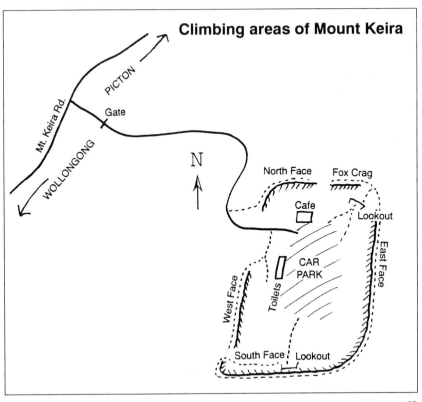

Climbing areas of Mount Keira

Location and Access

Mount Keira is located 10km north-west of the city of Wollongong, 80km south of Sydney on the east coast. Once in Wollongong, 82km down the Princess Highway, turn right onto Mount Keira Road, heading for Picton. Turn right again after a few kms up to the Mount Kiera lookouts. All the climbing areas are a short walk from the car park on the summit, where there are also toilets and a café. For the north face (hard sport routes) walk back down the road from the car park to find a track leading off right to the base of the cliff. For the west face (most popular area) again walk back down the road taking a vague track to the left before the road bends right. For the south face (also popular) follow the track from the car park to the south lookout, turning right down a track just before the lookout. For the east face take the track to the main lookout (north), climb down concrete steps, then scramble down to the base of the cliffs. The east face is to the right.

Camping and Supplies

Camping is not permitted at Mount Keira. There are several camping areas within the region. For more information contact the Wollongong tourist information centre in the town centre. Tel (042) 28 0300. Being the state's third largest city ample supplies are available here.

Climate and when to go

As with Nowra, Mount Keira has different areas facing in different directions, creating similar, year round climbing. Just choose the face you think will be best according to the conditions and time of day.

What to take

1 x 50m rope, standard rack of natural pro, 5 bolt plates.

Recommended classics

Fizzgig	15m	24	(North face)
Wallyard	20m	21	(North face)
Putain de Pudding	10m	25	(West face)
The Fixer	13m	21	(West face)
Hernia	10m	20	(West face)
Brigetta	10m	11	(West face)
Piece of Piss Direct	7m	15	(West face)
Upward Progress	6m	17	(West face)
Strong Arms	8m	16	(South face)
Mind Games	20m	16	(South face)
Travail	20m	13	(South face)

Useful information

For more information about climbing at Mt. Keira contact Hangdog Climbing Gym, 130 Aurburn Street, Wollongong 2500. Tel (042) 258 369. The tourist information centre is on the corner of Coown and Kembla Streets, Wollongong. Tel (042) 28 0300.

Guide to climbs

Rockclimber's Guide to Nowra and Wollongong edited by Rod Young (1994)

POINT PERPENDICULAR

Point Perpendicular is one of Australia's top sea cliffs, certainly as far as the east coast is concerned. The marvellous coastal position provides some very atmospheric climbing.

> **Geology:** Sandstone
>
> **Number of climbs:** 100
>
> **Grade of climbs:** 16-26
>
> **Potential for new routes:** No
>
> **Rock Quality:** Good
>
> **Length of climbs:** 15-60m 1 & 2 pitch
>
> **Protection:** Natural pro, bolts
>
> **Predominant climbing style:** Faces, steep
>
> **SPORT**

Location and Access

Point Perpendicular is on the southern tip of the Beecroft Peninsula, 35km south-east of Nowra. From Nowra drive 24km east along Currarong Road following the signs towards Currarong. Just before the township of Currarong, turn right (south) along the unsealed Lighthouse Road. Park at the end of this road after 10km where the lighthouse is reached. The climbing can be found on most of the cliffs around this southern tip. A lot of the climbs require an abseil to reach the base of the cliffs.

Camping and Supplies

Camping is not allowed at the lighthouse car park and it is important that climbers respect this ruling so the already tense access agreements are not endangered. Good camping is available at Honeymoon Bay, a NPWS administered camp about 7km from the climbing on the shores of Jervis Bay (see map). Supplies are best acquired from the town of Nowra as Currarong is limited.

Climate and when to go

Year round climbing is possible at Point Perpendicular, though spring (Sept-Nov) and autumn (Feb-May) have the most agreeable conditions. At other times of the year things can get a little too exiting due to the remorseless exposure of the elements.

What to take

Full rack of nuts and friends, snorkel and mask for great swimming at Jervis Bay.

Useful information

Much of the area is used by the navy for target bombing practice so there is a real risk that if you stray off track you might step on an unexploded mine! Keeping to marked tracks, taking note of all warning signs and access restrictions, is an absolute must.

Author's rating *

Guide to climbs

For more information about climbing at Point Perpendicular contact Mountain Designs in Sydney (address given).

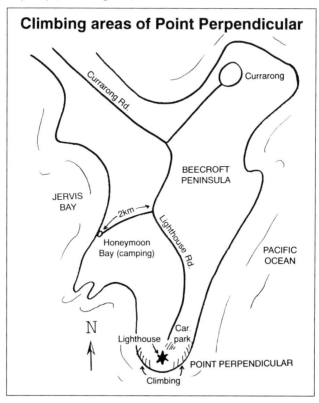

Climbing areas of Point Perpendicular

Useful addresses

City Crag (climbing gym)
Mountain Designs
499 Kent Street Sydney
NSW 2000
Tel (02) 267 3822

Grafton Climbing Wall
South Grafton Pool & Gym complex
77 Cambridge Street
South Grafton
NSW 2461
Tel (02) 42 3538

Lismore's Fit for All (gym)
81 Union Street, Lismore
NSW 2480
Tel (066) 21 8689

Rock Gym
9 Ador Avenue (in Police Citizen's
Youth Club), Rockdale
NSW 2216
Tel (02) 567 7631

Sydney Indoor Climbing Gym
59 Liverpool Road
Summer Hill
NSW 2130
Tel (02) 716 8949

The Climbing Centre
Unit 3, 16 Borec Road Penrith
NSW 2750
Tel (047) 3 1 1130

The Edge Indoor Climbing Centre
Unit 10, 5 Sailsbury Road
Castle Hill
NSW 2154
Tel (02) 899 8228

The Rocknasium
2/65-75 Captain Cook Drive
Carringbah
NSW 2229
Tel (02) 524 3944

Mountain Designs (Bouldering only)
190 Katoomba Street, Katoomba
NSW 2780
Tel (047) 82 5999

Hangdog Climbing Gym
130 Auburn Street, Wollongong
NSW 2500
Tel (042) 258 369

Climbfit
Unit 4, 12 Frederick Street
St Leonards, Sydney, NSW
Tel (02) 436 4600

Northern Beaches Roadhouse (gym)
19A Roger Street, Brookvale
NSW 2100
Tel (02) 905 6202

Tourism New South Wales Travel Centre
The MLC Building
19 Castlereagh Street, Sydney
NSW 2000
Tel (02) 231 4444

National Park & Wildlife Office
Cadman's Cottage & Information Centre
110 George Street, Sydney
NSW 2000
Tel (02) 247 8861

There is a good selection of outdoor
and equipment shops on Kent Street in
the city centre (Sydney).

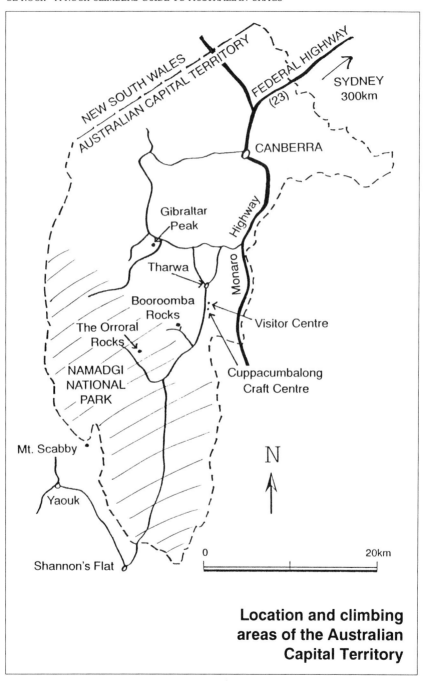

**Location and climbing
areas of the Australian
Capital Territory**

AUSTRALIAN CAPITAL TERRITORY

The Australian Capital Territory is a tiny state within New South Wales, 250km south-west of Sydney. Housing the country's capital, Canberra, the ACT is best known for politics and diplomatic events. However, there are topics of debate that will appeal to climbers, such as leadership issues associated with who gets to go first on some of Australia's finest granite.

BOOROOMBA ROCKS

This is what climbing in the ACT is all about. The smooth buttresses of Booroomba Rocks are a haven for traditional climbing, with many a middle grade classic on natural lines, all set in the pleasant and pleasing landscape of the Namadgi National Park.

Geology: Granite

Number of climbs: 300

Grade of climbs: 9-25

Potential for new routes: No

Rock quality: Good (can be abrasive)

Protection: Natural pro and bolts

Length of climbs: 10-180m single pitch

Predominant climbing style: Slabs, faces, cracks

SPORT

Location and Access

To reach Booroomba Rocks, find the town of Tharwa about 30km south of Canberra. Turn off to the right 10km along the Nass Road south of Tharwa onto Apollo Road, towards the Honeysuckle Creek Tracking Station. In 5km turn right again up a dirt road about 400m before the tracking station. Parking for the rocks is a short distance away at the end of this road. The main area of Booroomba consists of three buttresses (South Buttress, Middle Rocks and Northern Buttress). These are all within easy reach of each other, once the strenuous 20 minute uphill hike has been conquered.

Camping and Supplies

Some very nice camping is allowed at the base of the hill near the car park. There are no facilities. Ensure as little human impact is made as possible, and take your own water. The general store in Tharwa is the nearest place to Booroomba for your daily bread. The other option of course is the city of Canberra. The Cuppacumbalong craft centre near the visitors' information centre on Nass Road has a great variety of refreshments.

Climate and when to go

Using meteorological judgement, climbing is possible at any time of year, although more appealing conditions are in spring (Sept-Nov) and autumn (Feb-May). With the rocks at 1300m winter is cold and snow is a possibility.

What to take

Although there are good bolted routes, Booroomba is best known for its naturally protected climbs. Take a rack of natural gear, lots of wires and RPs for most routes, the odd friend, 2 x 50m ropes for multi-pitch leading, chalk to help protect fingertips from what is often gritty rock, drinking water.

Recommended classics

Integral Crack	19	(South Buttress)
Kilowatt	24	(South Buttress)
Roy's Crack	14	(South Buttress)
Hurricane Cracks	14	(Hurricane Cracks wall, Middle Rocks)
Smash Palace	23	(North Buttress) 3 pitch
Only the Good Die Young	22	(North Buttress) 4 pitch
Morning Thunder	20	(Hurricane Cracks wall, Middle Rocks)
Beau Temps	24	(Hurricane Cracks wall, Middle Rocks)
Hermes	16	(North Buttress) 3 pitch
Incisor	19	(North Buttress) 3 pitch

Useful information

The Australian National University indoor climbing club, at the Sports Union building in the suburb of Acton, just west of the city centre, is a good place to meet local climbers and find out more information about climbing in the ACT.

Author's rating *

Guide to climbs

Granite Climbs in the ACT edited by Tony Wood (1976)
More Granite Climbs in ACT edited by Tim Chapman (1983)

GIBRALTAR PEAK, THE ORRORAL ROCKS, MOUNT SCABBY

These are all quality granite crags for a good alternative to Booroomba Rocks (see map p168).

Useful addresses

The Australian National University
  indoor climbing wall
The Sport's Union Building
Acton
Canberra
ACT

Canberra City YMCA (gym)
London Circuit
Civic
ACT 2601
Tel (06) 249 3733

Mountain Designs (equipment)
Canberra
Tel (06) 247 7488

Canberra Tourist Bureau
Northbourne Avenue
PO Box 673
Dickson
ACT 2602
Tel (06) 205 0044

Australian Nature Conservation Agency
PO Box 636
153 Emu Bank
Belconnen
ACT 2614
Tel (06) 250 0200

The Canberra Tourist Bureau
14 Martin Place
Sydney
NSW 2000
Tel (02) 233 3666

Alphabetical Listing of Crags